Helion & Company Limited
Unit 8 Amherst Business Centre
Budbrooke Road
Warwick
CV34 5WE
England
Tel. 01926 499 619
Email: info@helion.co.uk
Website: www.helion.co.uk
Twitter: @helionbooks
Visit our blog http://blog.helion.co.uk/

Text © David François 2020
Photographs: Unless stated otherwise, all the photographs used in this volume have been obtained in the form of prints from the Military Museum of Hanoi and the Vietnam News Agency, in the Socialist Republic of Vietnam. In turn, these were obtained from official sources in Czechoslovakia and abroad, including the Ministry of Defence in Prague, and various news agencies in the late 1960s and through the 1970s.
Artworks: © David Bocquelet, Luca Canossa, Tom Cooper & Anderson Subtil 2020

Designed and typeset by Farr out Publications, Wokingham, Berkshire
Cover design Paul Hewitt, Battlefield Design (www.battlefield-design.co.uk)
Printed by Henry Ling Limited, Dorchester, Dorset

Every reasonable effort has been made to trace copyright holders and to obtain their permission for the use of copyright material. The author and publisher apologise for any errors or omissions in this work, and would be grateful if notified of any corrections that should be incorporated in future reprints or editions of this book.

ISBN 978-1-913336-29-5

British Library Cataloguing-in-Publication Data
A catalogue record for this book is available from the British Library

All rights reserved. No part of this publication may be reproduced, stored in a retrieval system, or transmitted, in any form, or by any means, electronic, mechanical, photocopying, recording or otherwise, without the express written consent of Helion & Company Limited.

We always welcome receiving book proposals from prospective authors.

CONTENTS

Abbreviations		2
Preface		2
1	Introduction	2
2	Socialist Czechoslovakia	6
3	The Prague Spring	17
4	The Five Against Prague	24
5	The Road to Invasion	35
6	The Invasion	42
7	Normalisation	58
Selected Bibliography		69
Notes		69
Acknowledgements		72
About the Author		72

Note: The above map shows the borders of Europe as at the time of publication. Czechoslovakia of 1968 comprised of the territories of the present day Czech and Slovak Republics.

ABBREVIATIONS

APC	armoured personnel carrier	KSČ	Komunistická strana Československa (Communist Party of Czechoslovakia)
C-in-C	commander in chief		
CO	commanding officer	KSS	Komunistická strana Slovenska (Communist Party of Slovakia)
CoS	Chief of Staff		
CPSU	Communist Party of the Soviet Union	NATO	North Atlantic Treaty Organisation
ČSSR	Československá socialistická republika (Czechoslovak Socialist Republic)	NPT	Treaty on the Non-Proliferation of Nuclear Weapons
FRG	Federal Republic of Germany	NVA	Nationale Volksarmee (National People's Army, the Armed Forces of the GDR)
ČSLA	Československá lidová armáda (Czechoslovakian People's Army)		
GDR	German Democratic Republic	SNB	Sbor národní bezpečnost (National Security Corps)
GSFG	Group of Soviet Forces in Germany		
HQ	headquarters	StB	Státní bezpečnost (State Police)
KAN	Klub angazovaných nestraniku (Club of Committed Non-Party Members)	UN	United Nations
		US$	United States Dollar
KGB	Komitet gossoudarstvennoï bezopasnosti (Committee for State Security)	USSR	Union of Soviet Socialist Republics (also 'Soviet Union')
Km	kilometre	VDV	Vozdushno-desantnye Voyska (Soviet Airborne Forces)
		WTO	Warsaw Treaty Organisation

PREFACE

1968 was a hot year in the history of the 20th century: Paris was covered with barricades and France experienced the largest general strike in its history; students agitated in Germany and Italy and were massacred in October in Mexico City. The winds of revolt even touched the United States, where the Democratic Convention in Chicago saw violent clashes between police and demonstrators hostile to the Vietnam War. This wind was also blowing across the Iron Curtain, where students agitated in Poland and dissidents demonstrated in Moscow's Red Square; but nowhere was this more the case than in Czechoslovakia, where there was an attempt to build a socialism different from the model proposed and imposed by Moscow.

Prefiguring the Union of the Soviet Socialist Republics (USSR, also 'Soviet Union') in the 1980s with the pro-reformer Mikhail Gorbachev, Czechoslovakia in 1968 was the melting pot of an original political model combining Communist Party hegemony and political liberalism, collective ownership and the pursuit of profit. This search for a model of socialism peculiar to a country that was, before 1938 and the Nazi takeover, a parliamentary democracy and an industrialised nation provoked the largest military operation on European soil since 1945, Operation Danube. Within hours, hundreds of thousands of soldiers and thousands of armoured vehicles took control of the entire country.

Operation Danube had essentially two goals: one political and the other strategic. The political objective was to put an end to the reform process and to establish a government that faithfully followed the political line defined by Moscow. The military goal was the long-term deployment of Soviet troops in Czechoslovakia, thus strengthening the USSR's military presence in Central Europe.

The invasion of Czechoslovakia was used to maintain the cohesion of the Eastern Bloc around Moscow for 20 years. When, in the late 1980s, Gorbachev refused to intervene militarily in the Baltic Republics or in neighbouring countries, the entire Soviet system collapsed, demonstrating the lack of legitimacy of the communist governments and the close ties that had united them since the October Revolution.

1 INTRODUCTION

Czechoslovakia – which appeared on the maps as a quadrilateral surrounded to the north, west and east by mountains, while to the south the Bohemian Basin opened to the Hungarian Plain – was at the heart of Europe while its history was at the confluence of all the currents that agitated the continent. Its western part, Bohemia, was a bastion of the Slavic world sandwiched between Silesia and German-speaking Austria. At the end of the 11th century, the Bohemian principality, part of the Holy Roman Empire, became a kingdom. The court of its king was then a high place of culture, and the capital Prague was endowed in 1348 with the first German-language university, whose radiation extended throughout Central Europe.[1]

Bohemia was also at the heart of the religious conflicts tearing Europe apart at the end of the Middle Ages. It saw first, at the beginning of the 15th century, the development of the Hussite movement led by Jan Hus, who advocated a religious reform, and then the success of Protestantism, whereas after 1526 the region was under the sovereignty of the Habsburg Catholics.[2] That same year, Slovakia, which belonged to the Kingdom of Hungary, passed under the control of the Habsburgs.

It was in Prague in 1618 that the defenestration of Vienna's representatives by Czech Protestant nobles sparked the terrible Thirty Years' War. The Imperial victory at the Battle of White Mountain in 1620 allowed the Habsburgs to assert their control over Bohemia. They imposed the Counter-Reformation, and 90 percent of the population – who were Protestant – returned, often by force, to Catholicism. Habsburg domination was also accompanied by a desire to Germanise Czech society, while the Slovaks were victims of a policy of Magyarisation.

The French Revolution, and especially the Revolutions of 1848, caused a Czech and Slovak revival. This revival was primarily cultural, with the purification of the Czech language of any Germanisms and a codification of the Slovak language in 1847. On the political level, Czechs demanded that their language be recognised with the same rights as the German one and called for an administrative decentralisation. The Czech national movement continued to develop throughout the 19th century, causing fear among the region's German population, which represented one-third of the people in Bohemia and Moravia. Czechs wanted to maintain the indivisibility of the country and obtain the use of the Czech language in the population's relations with the administration. The Germans, on the other hand, were striving to create an autonomous German territory in Bohemia and to divide the whole administration into Czech and German institutions, while keeping German as the official language. Czech cultural dynamism was reinforced by the industrialisation of the region, which was becoming an important economic centre. Slovakia, on the contrary, a region still largely rural, had more difficulty resisting Magyarisation, especially after the formation in 1867 of the Double Monarchy and despite the birth in 1871 of the Slovak National Party.

With the outbreak of the First World War, the leaders of the Czech national movement divided themselves between those who wished to take advantage of the conflict for Bohemia to enjoy a status of autonomy within the framework of the Austro-Hungarian Empire, and those who thought that only the Habsburgs' defeat would allow the creation of an independent Czech state. The latter, under the direction of Tomas Masaryk and Edvard Beneš, founded the Czechoslovak National Council in 1915, which settled in Paris. They were joined by the Slovak Milan Stefanik.[3] The Council was gradually recognised by Allied governments as representing the interests of the Czechs and Slovaks. To support these independentist demands, it relied on the creation of different military units. The Czechoslovak Legions were created in Russia in 1917, in France in December 1917 – including volunteers from America – and in Italy in April 1918. The soldiers were mainly ex-prisoners of war in Russia, Serbia and Italy, as well as emigrants from France and Russia. The Czechoslovak Legion in Russia played a crucial role in the Civil War after the Bolsheviks seized power in 1917.

The Czechoslovak Republic

In October 1918, when the Austro-Hungarian Empire disintegrated, the Czechoslovak Republic was proclaimed. Its first steps were chaotic since the Hungarians refused to leave the territory of Slovakia, which they called Upper Hungary. It was not until the demise of the Hungarian Soviet Republic in April 1919 that the Czechoslovak State could impose its authority in Slovakia. The borders of the new state were definitively fixed by the peace treaties of Versailles and Saint-Germain.

The country adopted a democratic constitution in 1920 with the election by universal suffrage of a Chamber of Deputies and a Senate. The parliamentarians elected the president of the Republic for a period of seven years. The first president was Tomas Masaryk, who was re-elected in 1927 and 1934 before resigning in 1935, being replaced by Edvard Beneš (sometimes anglicised to Edward Benesh). In 1920, Czechoslovakia joined the Little Alliance with Romania and Yugoslavia, under the auspices of France. This regional alliance was part of France's strategy of encircling Germany. The French helped to organise the Czechoslovak Army, which was trained by French officers. The army's Chief of Staff (CoS) would be, until 1924, a French general. On 25 January 1924, a military agreement was signed between the two countries, confirmed on 16 October 1925 by a promise of military assistance. In 1935, Prague also signed a military agreement with the Soviet Union against Germany.

This system of alliance ensured the internal stability of the country, which was deeply divided by national issues. Living within the borders of Czechoslovakia were Hungarian, Ruthenian, Polish and, above all, German minorities. The latter was the majority in certain regions, particularly in the Sudetenland, where a movement was developing in favour of making the area part of Germany. After coming to power in 1933, Hitler supported the claims of the Sudeten Germans and demanded their annexation to the Reich.

Czechoslovakia, convinced that it was supported by the Western democracies, rejected Nazi demands. The leaders of France and Great Britain did not have the stomach for a conflict in Europe however, and at Munich in September 1938 they concluded an agreement with Germany and Italy which led to the dismemberment of Czechoslovakia. In early October 1938, Germany occupied the Sudetenland, while Poland seized the region of Cieszyn and Hungary the southern areas of Slovakia and Ruthenia. By the end of 1938, Czechoslovakia had lost one-third of its territory and its population, more than 40 percent of its industry, a significant share of its raw materials and had become completely dependent on Germany.[4] On 14 March 1939, in agreement with Berlin, Slovak separatists announced the creation of an independent Slovak State, and the following day, German troops completed the occupation of the Czech regions, which were transformed by decree of Hitler into the Protectorate of Bohemia and Moravia.

President Beneš, who refused to recognise the 1938 Munich Agreement, emigrated first to Paris and then to London, where he formed a National Liberation Committee, which later became a Provisional Government. This government-in-exile was recognised in subsequent years by the Allied powers. Beneš and the Czechs also set up armed forces fighting in Poland in 1939, then in France in 1940. Czechoslovak pilots served in the RAF during the Battle of Britain, while the 11th Infantry Battalion-East fought in North Africa with the British Army and the 1st Czechoslovak Armoured Brigade participated in the liberation of France in 1944 as part of the 1st Canadian Army.[5]

The Czechoslovak Government in London signed a military cooperation agreement with the USSR on 18 July 1941 providing for the re-establishment of Czechoslovakia within its 1938 borders. On the basis of this agreement, Czechoslovak officers present in the Soviet Union were instructed at the end of 1941 to create military units there. The formation of the 1st Czechoslovak Infantry Battalion began in January 1942 in the city of Buzuluk, in the Orenburg region of southeast Russia. The battalion began to fight with the Red Army in March 1943 during a battle near the village of Sokolovo, in the

Kharkov region, and distinguished itself during the liberation of Kiev. In April 1944, the unit became the 1st Czechoslovak Army Corps under Colonel Ludvík Svoboda. On 6 October 1944, the corps, after fighting in Ukraine, reached the Carpathian Mountains with troops of the Soviet 38th Army of the 1st Ukrainian Front, seized the Dukel Pass and entered Slovak territory.[6]

Inside the former Czechoslovakia, non-communist resistance groups joined forces in the spring of 1940 to form the Central Directorate of the Resistance, which gradually shifted from distributing leaflets and a clandestine press to the collection of political and military information to be sent to London and also to Moscow. After the attack of the USSR by German troops in June 1941, these groups began a rapprochement with the Czechoslovak Communist Party (Komunistická strana Československa, or KSČ), but effective repression following the assassination of Reinhard Heydrich – the Nazi Deputy Protector of Bohemia and Moravia, and an architect of the Holocaust – in Prague in June 1942 marked a break in the unification process. The internal resistance struggled to recover from this wave of repression, and it was only towards the end of the war that it would recover completely. On 12 December 1943, Beneš signed an alliance between Czechoslovakia and the USSR, facilitating the unification of resistance forces. The Communist Resistance was then led from Moscow by Klement Gottwald and Rudolf Slanský, and animated on the spot by activists like Jan Sverma, Jaromír Dolanský, Antonin Novotný, Josef Smrkovský and Antonin Zapotocky.

While the urbanised, largely flat Bohemia offered little opportunity for guerrilla warfare, the situation was different in rural and mountainous Slovakia, where a partisan movement grew with the aid of Soviet support. Partisans trained in the USSR were parachuted into Slovakia in March 1944, along with Soviet officers, around whom were formed partisan units of several hundred fighters, such as the 1st Partisan Brigade Stefanik or the Jan Hus Brigade. The latter, which had more than 600 fighters in August 1944 under the leadership of a Soviet captain, also included former prisoners of war belonging to several European armies.[7]

When Bratislava was liberated by the Red Army, Beneš flew back from London, via Moscow, landing in Košice on 5 April 1945 and forming a coalition government headed by Zdeněk Fierlinger, with Klement Gottwald as first vice-president. The coalition was united by the Košice Programme, which provided for the creation of a democratic republic. Partisan warfare intensified as Allied armies advanced into Czechoslovakia. On 5 May, an uprising broke out in Prague. More than 1,600 barricades had been set up in the city, and some 30,000 men and women fought for three days against 37,000 Wehrmacht soldiers supported by tanks and artillery. Most of the country was liberated by Soviet and Romanian troops, with the exception of southwest Bohemia, which was overrun by the Western Allies. At the beginning of May, American troops reached Pilsen, while the Red Army entered Prague on 9 May. Fighting continued against the last German units until 11 May.

From liberation to Prague Coup

Throughout the regions of Central and Eastern Europe liberated by the Soviets, the situation in Czechoslovakia was unique. Prague had a Beneš-led government recognised by the Western Allies, and Soviet forces evacuated its territory in November 1945. With the communists having more than 700,000 militants in their ranks, Stalin asked Gottwald to get along with Beneš. A National Front of the Czechs and Slovaks was created, bringing together, besides the communists, the Social Democratic Party of President Beneš, the National Socialist Party of Czechoslovakia and the National Party. Slovakia had its own

Klement Gottwald, leader of the Communist Party of Czechoslovakia from 1929 until 1953, was elected as the first Communist president of Czechoslovakia in 1948, four months before his party seized a power through a Soviet-backed coup. (Bundesarchiv)

Edvard Beneš, president of Czechoslovakia from 1935 to 1938, leader of the Czechoslovak government-in-exile during the Second World War, and then president of the liberated country from 1945 to 1948. After suffering two strokes in 1947, he was in poor health and unable to effectively resist the Communist domination. (Bundesarchiv)

National Front, which included two parties, the Slovak Communist Party (Komunistická strana Slovenska, or KSS) and the Democratic Party, firmly established among the peasants, an important factor in agrarian Slovakia.

The new Czechoslovak authorities, and with the support of the population, very quickly proceeded with the mass expulsion of some three million German people, while in February 1946, Czechoslovakia and Hungary signed an agreement for the exchange of population on a parity basis. In the economic sphere, on 24 October 1945, Beneš, under pressure from the left wing, signed a law for the nationalisation of industry. The mining, metallurgy and energy sectors became the property of the State, while the chemical, metallurgical and textile

One of the armed communist militias on the streets of Prague in 1948.

sectors were partially nationalised. Only small businesses remained private. An agrarian reform had also been developed: in its first stage, land belonging to expelled Germans and Hungarians was divided and shared among the peasants.

On 26 May 1946, in the parliamentary elections, the Communist Party won in the Czech regions with 43.26 percent of the votes, while the Democratic Party won in Slovakia. Communists and Social Democrats won 151 seats out of 300 in parliament, but no party held a majority. However, the communists, as the most powerful party, formed a government and filled nine out of 26 ministerial positions. While they were in a minority in the government, they now held three key positions: Gottwald was Prime Minister (with extensive powers), the Interior Minister was Václav Nosek and Defence Minister was General Svoboda.[8] Under their guidance, a law was passed on 28 October 1946 installing a planned economy, while the agrarian reform was extended.

Despite measures taken by the government, Czechoslovakia was hit by a serious economic crisis in 1947. Gottwald was forced to reduce the distribution rate of food on ration cards by about 20 percent, leading to increased speculation and widespread discontent. The US government then refused to grant loans to Prague, forcing the Czechs to choose their side in the developing Cold War and to protest against nationalisation. While the Czech government tried to act as a pivot between the two emerging blocs, the announcement of the Marshall Plan in July 1947 put an end to any possible opening towards the West. While initially approved unanimously by the government in Prague, the plan was finally rejected a few days later. Czechoslovakia was now clearly allied with the Soviet Union, which reinforced its ideological and political influence over the country. On 11 December 1947, the first long-term trade agreement between the USSR and Czechoslovakia was concluded.

In early 1948, as the Cold War set in across Europe, Czechoslovakia became increasingly divided due to the growth of KSČ influence. A government crisis began on 19 February 1948, when non-communist parties decided to resign their ministers to protest against the activities of the Interior Minister, who had filled the police ranks with KSČ militants. The next day, at a government meeting, 12 liberal ministers announced their resignation in the hope that this would lead to the downfall of the Gottwald government and result in early parliamentary elections.

To protest against the resignation of the bourgeois ministers, the KSČ Central Committee called for a one-day general strike and, in agreement with the labour unions, appointed a congress of representatives of the country's trade unions, whose delegates were to arrive in Prague to support the actions of the government. At the same time, communist armed militia detachments started arriving in Prague, Bratislava and other cities. In addition, Czechoslovak communists who had been abroad – where they had received military training in the ranks of the resistance against the Nazis – were organised in special groups and took control of communications centres, radio stations, airports, bourgeois parties' HQs and the largest non-communist newspaper buildings. The police and the military did not interfere with what was happening, as the security forces were under the orders of Interior Minister Nosek, while the Army was led by Svoboda, who was close to the Soviets. On 25 February, while the whole country awaited the decision of President Beneš, a demonstration held in Prague attracted some 200,000 people and the workers' militias took control of key facilities around the city.[9]

Beneš finally accepted the resignation of the liberal ministers, who were replaced by communists and their social-democratic allies. The parliament approved the new government, and new parliamentary elections gave the majority to the Communist Party. On 9 May, a new constitution was promulgated, in which were inscribed the principle of the dictatorship of the proletariat and the dominant role of the Communist Party. Beneš, refusing to sign it, resigned on 7 June. Gottwald replaced him as President of the Republic, leaving the head of government to Zápotocký.

2 SOCIALIST CZECHOSLOVAKIA

The victory of the communists in 1948 inaugurated the transformation of Czechoslovakia into a socialist state on the Soviet model. The KSČ imposed its political domination, the economy was transformed and society was subjected by terror. At the international level, Prague aligned itself with Moscow in the fight against the West and actively supported the French and Italian communists.[1] With the risk that the Cold War in Europe could turn into an actual military conflict, the Czechoslovak armed forces were equipped and organised by the Soviet Army and integrated in the Warsaw Treaty Organisation (WTO) in 1955, in which they became one of the main pillars facing the Federal Republic of Germany (FRG) and North Atlantic Treaty Organisation (NATO).

Czechoslovakia from Gottwald to Novotný

After February 1948, Czechoslovakia became part of the Eastern Bloc and one of the political satellites of the Soviet Union. Czechoslovak communists began the construction of a socialist state. Politically, the new government turned its back on liberal democracy, while on 27 June 1948, the KSČ and the Social Democratic Party were merged into a single Marxist organisation, which retained the name KSČ.

Although, as in the rest of the communist world, Czechoslovakia adopted a government, a parliament and a President of the Republic, it was the KSČ which directed and governed the country. Its governing body was the Congress, which met every five years, but in reality it merely ratified decisions taken by the leadership and the list of members of the Central Committee presented to it. The Central Committee, consisting of about 100 members and 40 candidate members, led the party between Congresses. At the head of the KSČ was the General Secretary, who headed the Presidium and the Secretariat. The Presidium, chosen by the Central Committee and which included 11 members and two candidate members, determined the political line, while the Secretariat with its 11 members, some of which were also members of the Presidium, was responsible for overseeing the implementation of party policy. The KSČ's authority extended to the local level through the regional and local party committees. In Slovakia, the KSS was theoretically autonomous but in reality totally subordinated to the KSČ.

In the inter-war period, Czechoslovakia had been one of the most developed countries in the world, and in the Eastern Bloc after 1945, it was – with the German Democratic Republic (GDR) – the only state to present all the indicators of an industrialised country.[2] However, after February 1948, Prague reoriented its economy according to the needs of the USSR. A new land reform was decided, which limited land ownership to 50 hectares, while in industry, less than a third of companies remained private. The collectivisation of agriculture introduced repressive conditions that led to a decline in production. The resistance of the peasants to collectivisation necessitated the prolongation of the system of food cards until June 1953.

With agriculture and trade neglected, heavy industry became the economic priority for Czechoslovak leaders. The development of heavy industry was initially a response to the Soviet fears of a future conflict between East and West, but iron, coal and machinery were also – in the Stalinist ideology – the essential foundations of the construction of socialism.[3] Moreover, after the uncertainty of the 1950s, as the risk of world war decreased, heavy industry remained a key sector. In a country relatively poor in raw materials, such a development choice was naturally accompanied by a decline in economic efficiency, while centralised planning caused many problems, including breaks in the supply of the retail network, even for basic food products. These dysfunctions and the shortage of consumer goods were causing significant discontent among the population, particularly in the middle class.

As in the other Eastern Bloc countries, the break between Tito and Stalin in 1948 resulted in purges in the KSČ and the introduction of repressive measures by Czechoslovak security services, the StB (Státní bezpečnost, or State Police), organised with the help of KGB (Komitet gossoudarstvennoï bezopasnosti, or Committee for State Security) advisers. In November 1949, individuals such as the Deputy Minister of Foreign Trade, the editor-in-chief of the *Rude Pravo* – the KSČ Party newspaper – and the Prime Minister's adviser on economic affairs were arrested. The KSS was accused of 'deviationism' and 'nationalism'. Gustáv Husák, Chairman of the Council of Commissioners in Bratislava, and several of his associates were arrested in 1951. In the autumn 1952, Rudolf Slansky, the KSČ's General Secretary, was arrested before being executed in Bratislava, following a rigged trial.

Beyond the show trials that hit the KSČ leadership, all of Czechoslovak society was exposed to repression for political, social, professional or religious reasons. The victims were subjected to torture and extortion. While some were sentenced to death, most were imprisoned in labour camps that covered the whole country, such as Jachimov in northern Bohemia, where prisoners were subjected to forced labour in the uranium mine.[4]

However, Stalin's death in 1953 and Nikita Khrushchev's rise to power in Moscow led to the end of mass repression and opened a period of change. The 20th Congress of the Communist Party of the Soviet Union (CPSU) in 1956 denounced the 'cult of personality', condemning Stalin's policies and the Soviet Union's crimes during his reign. Under Khrushchev's leadership, the political trials of the 1950s

Anonín Josef Novotný, an ardent communist hardliner, and President of Czechoslovakia from 1957 until 1968.

were re-evaluated and the convicts rehabilitated. De-Stalinisation undermined the Eastern Bloc but did not provoke a popular movement in Czechoslovakia, as happened in the GDR in 1953 and in Hungary in 1956. Nevertheless, the new 'Khrushchevian' course and its denunciation of Stalinism quickly gave way in Czechoslovakia to more criticism about the country's situation.

On 14 March 1953, after his return from Stalin's funeral, President Gottwald died suddenly. He was replaced at the head of the state by Antonin Zápotocký, who reduced the pace of collectivisation in agriculture and announced in September 1953 a series of reforms to liberalise the economy. But Novotný, the KSČ leader, believed that these reforms did not go far enough: he wanted the end of collectivisation. To resolve the conflict that cracked the top of the Czechoslovak state, a delegation went to Moscow in April 1954. The Soviets stood unequivocally alongside Novotný, reprimanding Zapototcky for disobeying the Party leader. Novotný, meanwhile, demonstrated his loyalty to Khrushchev and de-Stalinisation.

On 13 November 1957, after the death of Zapotocky, Novotný became the new President while continuing to run the KSČ. As Krushchev's loyal supporter, he dismantled Stalin's monument in Prague, supported the Kremlin in its condemnation of Albania and China, and launched a campaign to rehabilitate a number of victims of the purges of the early 1950s.[5] In 1960, he declared a widespread amnesty for political prisoners and at the same time announced the "final construction of socialism" in Czechoslovakia, after which the country, formerly known as the Czechoslovak Republic, was renamed the Czechoslovak Socialist Republic (Československá socialistická republika, or ČSSR). Nevertheless, Novotný kept intact the political system whereby the KSČ still tightly controlled the economic, social, political and cultural life of the country.

The primary tank of the Czechoslovak People's Army in the 1950s was the venerable T-34/85. Very few were still in service as of 1968.

The Czechoslovak People's Army

Czechoslovakia's transition into the socialist camp from 1948 onwards meant its integration into the military and strategic system led by the USSR. At the end of the Second World War, the Czechoslovak Army had to fulfil various missions, such as the struggle against the Ukrainian separatists in Slovakia, the expulsion of the German population from the Sudetenland and economic reconstruction, which prevented it from developing its capabilities to fight.

It was therefore an army in the process of reconstruction when Alexej Čepička became the new Communist Defence Minister in June 1950. According to historian Karel Kaplan, Čepička was ordered by Stalin personally to prepare the Czechoslovak Army for an incursion into Western Europe.[6] He launched a radical reform of the armed forces, with the help of Soviet military advisers led by Colonel General Gusev. In September 1951, 73 Soviet military advisers worked in Czechoslovakia at different levels of the army. By 1955, the number of these advisers had increased to 264. At the same time, officers whose loyalty to the new government was in doubt were dismissed and new officers were recruited.[7]

The challenge for the communist power was to make the armed forces an instrument that demonstrated obedience and loyalty to the KSČ. It also changed their name in 1954 to become the Czechoslovakian People's Army (Československá lidová armáda, or ČSLA), an army entirely subordinate to the KSČ. The ČSLA's organisation and its missions were the sole responsibility of the KSČ Presidium. Its orientation was defined at the congresses and meetings of the KSČ Central Committee, which sought to uphold the Leninist principles of building socialist armed forces, including the leading role

Czechoslovak industry and the armed forces pressed into service numerous domestic variants of German armament manufactured in local factories during the Second World War. Amongst these were OT-810s, based upon the famous German SdKfz.251 half-track. Some 1,500 of these were manufactured by Praga and Tatra between 1958 and 1962.

Table 1: ČSLA in 1968[10]	
Western Military District	**Příbram**
1st Tank Division	Slaný
13th Tank Division	Mladá
2nd Motorised Rifle Division	Sušice
19th Motorised Rifle Division	Pilsen
20th Motorised Rifle Division	Karlovy Vary
311th Heavy Artillery Brigade	Stará Boleslav
322nd Artillery Brigade	Strašice
216th Anti-Tank Regiment	Dobřany
259th Anti-Aircraft Brigade	Pilsen
1st Radio Battalion Radio	Stříbro
51st Engineer Brigade	Litoměřice
73rd Bridge Battalion	Kostelec nad Labem
91st Bridge Battalion	Terezin
105th Chemical Protection Regiment	Liberec
1st Liaison Regiment	Beroun
71st Communication Battalion	Litomerice
1st Radar Regiment	Kolín
2nd Automobile [Transport] Brigade	Bílina
4th Artillery Base	Terezin
3rd Tank Base	Luštěnice
4th Tank Base	Stráž pod Ralskem
Central Military District	**Tábor**
4th Tank Division	Havlíčkův Brod
9th Tank Division	Písek
3rd Motorised Rifle Division	Kromeriz
15th Motorised Rifle Division	České Budějovice
321st Heavy Artillery Brigade	Rokycany
332nd Artillery Brigade	Jičín
33rd Anti-Tank Brigade	Lešany
82nd Anti-Aircraft Brigade	Jaroměř
260th Anti-Aircraft Brigade	Brno
4th Radio Battalion	Drhovice
1st Engineer Brigade	Pardubice
72nd Bridge Battalion	Kamýk nad Vltavou
101st Chemical Protection Regiment	Jaroměř
103rd Chemical Protection Regiment	Červená Voda
2nd Communication Regiment	Tábor
5th Communication Regiment	Pardubice
74th Communication Battalion	Horažďovice
1st Automobile [Transport] Brigade	Vysoké Mýto
2nd Artillery Base	Jaroměř
1st Tank Base	Vyškov
Eastern Military District	**Trenčín**
14th Tank Division	Prešov
220th Anti-Tank Regiment	Topolčany

Units directly subordinated to the Military Defence Committee	
331st Heavy Artillery Brigade	Hranice
7th Airborne Regiment	Holešov
2nd Radio Regiment	Rožmitál pod Třemšínem
7th Special-Purpose Radio Regiment	Zbiroh
7th Liaison Regiment	Litomerice
52nd Cable Regiment	Lipnik nad Becvou
59th Communication Regiment	Prague
55th Cable Battalion	Nové Město nad Metují
5th Road Brigade	Liberec
31st Road Brigade	Česká Třebová
32nd Road Brigade	Horní Počáply
7th Bridge Brigade	Hodonin
1st Operational Brigade	Prague
4th Border Guard Brigade	Znojmo
5th Border Guard Brigade	Cheb
7th Border Guard Brigade	Sušice
9th Border Guard Brigade	Domažlice
11th Border Guard Brigade	Bratislava
12th Border Guard Brigade	Planá u Mariánských Lázní
15th Border Guard Brigade	České Budějovice
1st Gas Pipeline Brigade	Roudnice nad Labem

of the Communist Party, and loyalty to proletarian internationalism, which meant respect for the Soviet alliance.

No political party other than the KSČ could exist in the armed forces, and in the 1960s, the ČSLA was politicised by a communist ideology and subjected to a pro-Soviet orientation. The highest national political body in military matters was the Military Defence Committee of the KSČ Central Committee, while an official political apparatus was built within the ČSLA. This main political administration of the ČSLA was headed by a member of the Defence Ministry who was also a member of the KSČ Central Committee. It was composed of politically trained professional soldiers engaged by the KSČ. Their task was important, since military service was conceived as a means of ideological influence on the majority of the male population through the political education received by each recruit.[8]

The 1950s were marked by an important development of the Czechoslovak military forces. The ČSLA's organisation was based on division of the territory into three military districts – the Western, Central and Eastern. In the early 1950s, the ČSLA comprised 170,000 men in 14 divisions, including two mechanised and two armoured. This number increased in the first half of the 1950s when the Cold War rose in intensity, reaching some 250,000 men.[9] In 1958, they were reduced to 182,000 men in 11 divisions, including three armoured. In the second half of the 1960s, the ČSLA still had 14 divisions, most of which were located in the western part of the country.

The Soviet influence on the ČSLA covered all areas, including matériel.[11] In the late 1940s, the Czechoslovak Army was equipped with British tanks such as the Cromwell IV and VI,

An IS-3 heavy tank of the Czechoslovak People's Army, seen on the streets of Prague during a parade in the early 1960s.

During the 1960s, the locally-manufactured variant of the T-54 became the standard main battle tank of the Czechoslovak People's Army.

Stuart and Challenger alongside Soviet T-34/76 and T-34/85 tanks. In the following years, most of the ČSLA matériel was of Soviet origin. It received T-54 tanks in the early 1950s. From 1956, T-54 tanks were even manufactured in Czechoslovakia.

The same phenomenon affected the Czechoslovak Air Force, which was rebuilt in early 1944 with Lavochkin La-5FNs and La-5UTIs. These equipped two fighter regiments of the I Czechoslovak Corps, which fought in the Red Army but also flew Supermarine Spitfire Mk.IXs. Little by little, the British fighters were replaced by Soviet fighters such as the La-7, which remained in service until 1950.

Czechoslovak Aerospace Industry

The Czechoslovaks were also developing their own aerospace industry. For example, the Avia factory in Prague-Čakovice, which assembled Messerschmitt Bf.109G fighter during the Second World War, continued production with the Messerschmitt Bf-109G-14, which received the S-99 designation, and the Bf-109G-12, renamed CS-99. Fighters were also built by installing bomber engines in the Bf-109, resulting in the model named Avia S-199. About 600 S-199s were built until 1949, 25 of which were sold to Israel, and these fighters remained in service with the Czechoslovak Air Force until the mid-1950s. Meanwhile, the Avia factory began manufacturing S-92 and CS-92 jet fighters, based on the Messerschmitt Me.262. The first S-92 flight took into the air at the end of August 1946, and all available S-92s and CS-92s were integrated in the 5th Fighter Squadron, where they remained in service until 1951.

Soviet Equipment for the Air Force

Many squadrons were created in the 1950s, new air bases were built and, of course, a large number of Czechoslovak pilots received training under the supervision of Soviet advisers. In 1950, 12 Yakovlev Yak-23s arrived in Czechoslovakia, and another 10 fighters of this type joined them at Mladá Boleslav air base. The capacity of the Czechoslovak Air Force increased considerably with the arrival of the Mikoyan-Gurevich MiG-15 fighter in 1951. This had very powerful weaponry, consisting of one 37mm and two 23mm guns, and strongly impressed the Czechoslovak pilots. Prague asked to be able to produce this fighter by buying a license. The serial assembly of the MiG-15, now called S-102, began in 1953 with the Aero Vodochody Company. Soon after, Czechoslovakian factories started building an improved MiG-15bis fighter under the designation S-103.

During the 1950s, the Czechoslovak Air Force became involved in several incidents with the air forces of NATO. The most famous was an incident known as the 'Merklin Air Battle': it occurred on 10 March 1953 in the western Pilsen region. In the first clash of the Cold War era between US Air Force and Soviet fighter jets in Europe, two US F-84E Thunderjet fighter-bombers entered Czechoslovak airspace from the FRG, in response to which Czechoslovak regional air defence command sent two MiG-15s to intercept them. The MiG-15s opened fire and damaged one Thunderjet. The Americans fighters, under fire, headed for the FRG, but the MiGs pursued them and shot down one of the American jets, which crashed in West Germany 20km south of Regensburg.

MiG-15 fighters remained in service until the end of the 1960s. They were gradually replaced by the MiG-17F from 1955 onwards: others were modified as fighter-bombers, receiving the local designation MiG-15bisSB, or for reconnaissance purposes, as MiG-15bisR. A small number of MiG-17Fs were provided directly by the USSR, with most of the fighters being built under licence by the Aero Vodochody factory, receiving the S-104 designation. A total of 457 MiG-17F and MiG-17PF jets were built in Czechoslovakia, remaining in service until the early 1970s.

In 1957, an agreement was reached on the delivery of 12 MiG-19S and 24 MiG-19P fighters to Czechoslovakia. The following year, another 12 MiG-19S were delivered by Moscow, and Czechoslovakia was the only country of the WTO to receive a license to build MiG-19Cs under the designation S-105 in 1959. In total, the Czechoslovak Air Force used 182 MiG-19 fighters, 79 of which were delivered by the USSR. Among these fighters were 33 MiG-19PM interceptors, received in 1960, which were used until July 1972. In response to the improvement of NATO fighter jets in the 1960s, Warsaw Pact air forces were equipped with supersonic MiG-21 delta-wing fighter jets. Indeed, Czechoslovakia, bordering West Germany, was one of the first Eastern Bloc countries to adopt the MiG-21F-13 fighter; in 1962, the first Soviet-built MiG-21F-13 entered service with the Czechoslovak Air Force. In the same year, licensed construction of this type began at the Aero Vodochody factory: some of these were modified for reconnaissance purposes, and received the designation MiG-21FR. Regarding its bomber fleet, the Czechoslovak Air Force was equipped with Ilyushin Il-28s in the 1950s and Sukhoi Su-7 fighter-bombers in the following decade.[12] The acquisition of Su-7s was of particular importance, because their primary role was that of nuclear strike.

A front view of a MiG-15bisSB fighter-bomber, with its 'arsenal', consisting of unguided rockets and 100kg bombs.

A radar-equipped MiG-17PF all-weather and night interceptor of the Czechoslovak Air Force: a 'great leap forward' of the second half of the 1950s, it was already essentially obsolete by the early 1960s.

One of 24 MiG-19S of the Czechoslovak Air Force acquired in 1957-1958.

Because no Soviet troops were stationed in Czechoslovakia, while the country bordered on the FRG and its 1st and 4th Armies required air support, a total of 107 Su-7BM and Su-7BKL fighter-bombers, and Su-7U two-seat conversion trainers were acquired: in the case of a war, they were to be armed with Soviet-owned and -handled tactical nuclear bombs, as necessary.[13]

As of 1968, the air force was re-organised as the Air Force Command, 10th Army of the Czechoslovak People's Army. At its forefront were one fighter aviation division with three fighter aviation regiments, and two fighter-bomber aviation divisions with three fighter-bomber aviation regiments (operating Su-7BKL/BMs and MiG-15bis/bisSBs), as listed in Table 2.

Besides the ČSLA, the KSČ had its own military force, the People's Popular Militia (Lidové milice), formed in 1948 and controlled by the KSČ Central Committee's 8th Department, which was also responsible for supervising the ČSLA.[15] Composed of communist militants, in 1968 it included 78,000 men who received basic military training and were divided into teams in more than 2,000 factories around the country.[16] Militia equipment was improved during the 1960s, when it received vz. 52 rifles, vz. 58 assault rifles and vz. 59 machine guns. It also had GAZ off-road trucks, along with R-108 and R-105 portable radios.[17] By the late 1960s, the ČSLA was a modern and numerous army, one of the main pillars of the Warsaw Pact in its face-off against NATO.

ČSLA in the Warsaw Pact Organisation

In 1955, in reaction to the formation of NATO, Eastern Bloc countries signed the Warsaw Pact: this defensive military alliance between seven countries stipulated that the armed forces of each state were integrated into a unified command.[18] The alliance was led by a Political Advisory Committee, which included key Communist Party leaders, heads of state and army commanders, who met to discuss international issues related to the common interests of member states.

A four-ship of MiG-21F-13s in full Czechoslovak markings and with launch rails for R-3S infra-red homing air-to-air missiles.

A total of around 100 Su-7BKL/BM fighter-bombers – capable of deploying tactical nuclear weapons – formed the backbone of the Czechoslovak Air Force in the late 1960s. In the foreground are two old FAB-250M-46 general-purpose bombs.

Table 2: Czechoslovak Air Force, 1968[14]		
10th Air Army	Hradec Kralove	
1st Fighter Aviation Division	Bechyne	
4th Fighter Aviation Regiment	Pardubice	MiG-21F-13 (2 squadrons), MiG-19PM (1 squadron)
5th Fighter Aviation Regiment	Líně	MiG-19S (2 squadrons), MiG-19PM (1 squadron)
9th Fighter Aviation Regiment	Bechyně	MiG-21F-13 (2 squadrons), MiG-21PFM (1 squadron)
2nd Fighter-Bomber Aviation Division	Přerov	
6th Fighter-Bomber Aviation Regiment	Přerov	MiG-15bis (3 squadrons)
20th Fighter-Bomber Aviation Regiment	Náměšť nad Celebration	Su-7BKL/BM (3 squadrons)
30th Fighter-Bomber Aviation Regiment	Hradec Králové	MiG-15B/bis (3 squadrons)
34th Fighter-Bomber Aviation Division	Čáslav	
2nd Fighter Bomber Aviation Regiment	Čáslav	MiG-15bis (3 squadrons)
18th Fighter-Bomber Aviation Regiment	Čáslav	MiG-15SB/bis (3 squadrons)
28th Fighter-Bomber Aviation Regiment	Čáslav	Su-7BKL/BM (3 squadrons)
46th Transport Aviation Division	Olomouc	
1st Airborne Regiment	Mosnov	Il-14T (3 squadrons), Mi-1, Mi-4 (1 squadron)
12th Helicopter Aviation Regiment	Olomouc	Mi-4 (3 squadrons)
24th Helicopter Aviation Regiment	Brno	Mi-4 (3 squadrons)
3rd Aviation Technical Division	Pardubice	
5th Aeronautical Technical Division	Olomouc	
10th Electronic Warfare Aviation Battalion	Přerov	Il-28RT/RTR, Il-14RT/RTR, Mi-1 (1 squadron)
45th Artillery Reconnaissance Aviation Regiment	Line	MiG-15bis/bisR (1 squadron), L-29/29R (2 squadrons)
47th Reconnaissance Aviation Regiment (directly subordinated to the General Staff 10th Air Army)	Mladá	MiG-21FR (1 squadron), Il-28R/28RT (1 squadron), MiG-15bis/bisR (2 squadrons)
50th Liaison Aviation Regiment	Kbely	
10th Liaison Regiment	Klecany	
7th Air Defence Army		
III Air Defence Corps	Zatec	
1st Fighter Aviation Regiment	České Budějovice	
11th Fighter Aviation Regiment	Zatec	
71st Anti-Aircraft Missile Brigade	Prague	
185th Anti-Aircraft Brigade	Kralovice	
51st Radio Battalion	Chomutov	
52nd Radio Battalion	Dobřany	
53rd Radio Battalion	České Budějovice	
54th Radio Battalion	Opatovice nad Labem	
II Air Defence Corps	Brno	
8th Fighter Aviation Regiment	Mosnov	
76th Anti-Aircraft Brigade	Brno	
77th Anti-Aircraft Brigade	Ostrava	
186th Anti-Aircraft Missile Regiment	Pezinok	
61st Radio Battalion	Brno	
62nd Battalion Radio	Ostrava	
63rd Battalion Radio	Trnava	
64th Battalion Radio	Zvolen	
17th Communication Regiment	Prague	

A MiG-21PFM landing while armed with RS-2U (ASCC/NATO-codename 'AA-1 Alkali') beam-riding air-to-air missiles.

An Il-28 light bomber of the Czechoslovak Air Force: by 1968, these were considered obsolete for front line duties and relegated to secondary purposes.

The Advisory Committee ratified collective decisions, particularly concerning the reinforcement of defence capabilities and in respect of the common obligations of members. As subsidiary bodies, there was also a Permanent Committee – which made recommendations for negotiations on foreign policy issues – as well as a joint secretariat to arrange regular agendas between Political Advisory Committee meetings.

The Warsaw Pact Joint Command, located in Moscow in the building of the General Staff of the Soviet Armed Forces, was formally responsible for shaping the decisions of the Political Advisory Committee on defence matters, managing the forces provided by the member states and implementing measures necessary for their security. The head of the WTO's armed forces had its own staff, but it was small, and the WTO's governing body was exclusively the Soviet General Staff. The latter was the only one that determined the use of Warsaw Pact armies in the event of war and their evolution in times of peace. The WTO Armed Forces C-in-C was also Deputy Minister of Defence of the USSR and was therefore directly subordinated to the Soviet Defence Minister. The WTO C-in-C was also Deputy Chief of the General Staff of the Soviet Armed Forces, to which he was directly subordinated. It was therefore Moscow that decided the strategic plans of the Warsaw Pact, the number of troops deployed, the number of divisions in peacetime, all their equipment and the progressive modernization of WTO armed forces.

In addition to the almost total control of its allies' armed forces, the Warsaw Pact had the advantage for the USSR of justifying the deployment of its troops in the GDR, Poland, Hungary and Romania. The Soviet Army was absent from Czechoslovakia, from which it withdrew at the end of 1945 before then leaving Bulgaria in 1947 and Romania in 1958, a country that had no border with an 'imperialist' state. Soviet forces deployed in Eastern Europe were divided between the Group of Soviet Forces in Germany (GSFG) in the GDR, the Northern Group of Forces in Poland and the Southern Group of Forces in Hungary: a total of nearly half a million soldiers.[19]

Czechoslovakia played a crucial role in the Warsaw Pact system. It was the link between Soviet forces north of its borders and those in Hungary, ensuring the smooth transfer of Soviet units between the north and south of the European 'battlefield' and their logistical support. Its western border was also the western border of the Warsaw Pact alliance, which thus put the country in the front line in case of war with the West. This strategic situation pushed Moscow to propose to Prague the deployment of two Soviet divisions in Czechoslovakia to correct the 'mistake' made in 1945 in withdrawing its troops from the country. But at the end of 1954, the Czechoslovak leaders rejected this offer.[20] The question of the presence of Soviet forces on Czechoslovak

Once Czechoslovakia joined the WTO, its forces were integrated with those of allied countries and ran regular joint exercises. This photograph shows a Mil Mi-1 helicopter of the Czechoslovak Air Force overflying a D-442 FUG amphibious armoured scout car of the Hungarian Army.

To eastern France in eight or nine days: a soldier of the ČSLA preparing a rocket propelled grenade for an RPG-7 anti-tank weapon.

soil thereafter became a sticking point between Moscow and Prague. For the Soviets, the absence of their troops in Czechoslovakia weakened this sensitive front against NATO, while the Czechoslovaks wanted to retain at last a remnant of their sovereignty.

The refusal to host Soviet divisions on its territory compelled Prague to strengthen the ČSLA, which had to increase its numbers and sped up its rearmament between 1955 and 1959. To achieve these goals, in January 1955, the KSČ Presidium decided to reorganise the ČSLA, extend basic military service for three years and modernise its armament. According to Soviet plans, in 1956, in the event of war, the ČSLA was to mobilise 760,000 combatants. Such an effort was difficult for a country with only 14 million inhabitants, and in October 1958 the required wartime numbers were reduced to 650,000, while peacetime numbers were cut to about 180,000 soldiers.[21] However, the ČSLA's operational tasks set by Moscow remained unchanged, so the lower number of soldiers had to be compensated for by greater firepower.

In the operational plans of the 1950s, the Soviets gave the ČSLA an essentially defensive role. According to Soviet instructions of May 1955, the ČSLA was tasked to not let enemy troops enter its territory at the beginning of the war in order to ensure the deployment of the main forces of the Warsaw Pact, and then to launch a counterattack on the southern FRG to a depth of 50–60km. This situation, however, changed as the Soviet military evolved their strategic designs in a resolutely offensive direction, based on the strength of conventional forces and the use of tactical and strategic nuclear weapons.[22] The 1961 Operational Plan therefore gave the ČSLA an offensive mission in case of conflict. The Berlin Crisis in 1961, followed by the Cuban Missile Crisis the following year, contributed to the changing of Soviet military doctrine, which definitively adopted the principle of limited nuclear war in Central Europe, as theorised by Marshal Sokolovskii in 1963. The Soviet doctrine became totally offensive, as shown in the 1964 WTO Operational Plan which provided for troops to advance 80–120km per day and the use of nuclear strikes. Consequently, between the seventh and eighth day of the war, the ČSLA had to reach the line Langres–Besançon in eastern France, a distance of some 600km.[23] Certainly enough, such an operation was expected to cause the loss of 60–70% of the ČSLA's manpower in a matter of few days, a prospect and sacrifice that frightened Czechoslovak military officers and undermined their confidence in the WTO.[24]

Czechoslovak political and military leaders were immediately sceptical about the possibilities of the ČSLA achieving the goals set by the Warsaw Pact. They were nevertheless willing to pay the price to avoid the presence of Soviet forces on their territory in peacetime, including the high cost of armaments. It soon became apparent, however, that there was a strong possibility of the Czechoslovak economy being unable to meet the military matériel needs for the tasks assigned by the Soviet Staff. Ambitious arms plans could only be partially achieved, and the command of the army had to considerably reduce its needs. However, between 1961 and 1965, some 28.4 billion korunas were spent to modernise the ČSLA's armament.[25] In 1965, the Czechs asked Moscow to reduce their obligations, including a reduction in the number of air regiments from 20 to 17, which would save 1.6 billion korunas.[26] Prague's inability to fulfil its commitments called into question the strategic plans of the WTO armies, but also suggested to Soviet leaders that Czechoslovakia was a weak point in their military apparatus.

For some historians, the excessive effort demanded of the ČSLA was only a clever means of forcing Prague to accept the installation of Soviet troops on its territory. They have put forward several arguments to support this thesis. First, the demands imposed by the Soviet Staff on the ČSLA exceeded those thrust upon other WTO

Due to the high pace of operations envisaged by Soviet planners, any ČSLA advance into the FRG would have required intensive aerial support. The seven helicopter squadrons of the 46th Transport Aviation Division of the Czechoslovak Air Force that were equipped with Mil Mi-4 helicopters – like the example in this photograph – were thus expected to play a highly important role in the case of a war with NATO.

armies. The number of troops mobilised by the ČSLA had far exceeded the effort required by the East German National Volksarmee (National People's Army, or NVA) or the Polish People's Army. After the Soviet Union, Czechoslovakia, with Bulgaria, had the highest per capita military spending in the Warsaw Pact.[27]

When the Czechoslovakians asked that the military effort demanded of them be reduced, the Soviets refused, and in 1967, new Russian leader Leonid Brezhnev compromised by asking the ČSLA to create facilities for the rapid arrival of Soviet air forces on its territory in the event of conflict. The Czechs recognised that their armed forces need to be reinforced by Soviet formations, and at a meeting in April 1967, the Soviets believed that only a risk of war would allow them to deploy their troops in Czechoslovakia.

MiG-21PFs were some of the most advanced jets of the Czechoslovak Air Force in 1968: while primarily deployed as interceptors (the example here has a launch rail for an R-3S air-to-air missile under its left wing), some were modified for deployment of nuclear weapons and had strike as their secondary role.

The question of the presence of Soviet troops in Czechoslovakia was a major concern for the Soviet General Staff. The 1964 Operational Plan provided for the use of nuclear weapons by the Czechoslovak Front, but the ČSLA did not have the means to develop its own nuclear weapons. Moscow, after its recent misadventure with China, wanted to keep its nuclear monopoly within the socialist camp. Since the late 1950s, the Soviets had been negotiating with the Americans to limit nuclear testing, establish non-proliferation and create nuclear-free zones. This process led to the signing of the Treaty on the Non-Proliferation of Nuclear Weapons (NPT) in June 1968, which prevented Moscow from deploying nuclear weapons in Prague.

To circumvent this problem, it was decided to deliver missiles and aircraft to the ČSLA, but without nuclear warheads, which would be provided by the Soviet Army only in case of conflict.[28] In March 1961, at a meeting of the Warsaw Pact Political Advisory Committee, Moscow confirmed the supply of 3R-9 Luna (FROG-3) tactical missiles to the ČSLA and R-11M and R-17 (SS-1C Scud A and B respectively) tactical operational missiles for tank and motorised rifle divisions. By 1968, the ČSLA had 28 R-11M and R-17 missiles and the same number of Luna carriers. On 19 July 1963, an international agreement had been signed for the supply of Sukhoi Su-7 fighter-

The supply of missile launchers and aircraft capable of carrying nuclear weapons appeared, however, to be insufficient for the Soviet military. They feared that the time needed to deliver nuclear warheads to the ČSLA would cause delays when launching an offensive against the West and threaten the left flank of the main assault from the GDR towards Paris. For them, only the presence of Soviet troops in Czechoslovakia could solve this problem, since the NPT allowed the presence of nuclear weapons on the territory of an allied country on the sole condition that they were under the control of the signatory country of the treaty. The Soviet Staff therefore again proposed the installation in Czechoslovakia of two divisions, which would justify the storage of nuclear weapons in the country. But the Czechoslovak leaders, including Novotný, once more refused the presence of Soviet units, fearing that this was a way for Moscow to influence domestic politics.[30] Nevertheless, a change in the leadership in Prague could help to break this deadlock.

A brand-new Su-7BM/BKL of the Czechoslovak Air Force, seen shortly after delivery. Notable is the lack of additional outboard underwing pylons and a rear-view mirror atop the cockpit transparency, making them easily distinguishable from better-known Su-7BMKs exported subsequently outside Europe.

bombers capable of carrying nuclear bombs. Between 1965 and 1967, 102 such aircraft were purchased and delivered in the Su-7BM, Su-7BKL and Su-7U versions. A dozen MiG-21PFMs delivered between 1966 and 1968 were also capable of carrying tactical nuclear bombs.[29] Soviet-controlled depots were built in Czechoslovakia to store the nuclear weapons that would be handed over to the ČSLA in the event of war.

3
THE PRAGUE SPRING

Czechoslovakia, a highly industrialised country and a showcase for communist efficiency, experienced a serious economic crisis in the early 1960s, while the lack of freedom in a society that had lived in a liberal democracy between 1918 and 1938 provoked discontent among much of the population. Alexander Dubček's attempt to find an alternative to the Soviet model for his country opened a Pandora's box that upset the foundations on which socialist Czechoslovakia was built, whilst arousing the fear and anger of Moscow and the WTO allies.

The fall of Novotný
Novotný, although a devotee of Khrushchev and his policy of de-Stalinisation, wanted to strictly control the process of liberalisation. He ran up against the opposition of the Slovaks, who criticised the over-strong centralisation of the Czechoslovak political system. The last remnants of Slovak autonomy were lost thanks to Stalinisation and purges within the KSS. The Slovak reformers linked the issue of de-Stalinisation to that of national autonomy. They were supported by Czech liberals, who were particularly active among intellectuals. Novotný managed to calm the Slovaks in 1963 by rehabilitating Husak, who resumed his position in the KSČ.[1] The rehabilitation of Slansky and Clementis, the restriction of the powers of censorship and the liberalisation of artistic activities facilitated contacts with the West and allowed the government to establish a *modus-vivandi* with the liberal opposition.[2] On the economic front, where the country was in difficulty, Novotný also had to make concessions and loosen the grip of economic planning. From 1965, the KSČ implemented economic reforms which raised in the population an aspiration for political changes.[3]

While Novotný's concessions were part of Khrushchev's policy, from the mid-1960s he had to take into account the ideological hardening expressed in Moscow when Brezhnev came to power in 1964. The end of the thawing policy caused opposition in the USSR. On 5 December 1965, at Pushkin Square in Moscow, a dissident demonstration was held, including Andrei Sakharov, Alexander Ginzburg and Vladimir Bukovsky, marking the birth of a human rights movement in the country. To stem this new opposition, the leadership of the Soviet Union resorted to repressive measures such as deprivation of citizenship and deportation abroad.

In Czechoslovakia, intellectuals were also at the forefront of opposition to the regime's inaction. They were heard at the Fourth Congress of the Czechoslovak Writers' Union, which was held on 27 and 29 June 1967. Discussions on the situation in society were at the centre of these debates. The bureaucratic governance style of Novotný was the target of keen criticism. In terms of foreign policy, the unconditional support of the Czechoslovak government for Soviet policy in the Middle East at the time of the Six-Day War and the anti-Semitic campaign launched at this time angered intellectuals because it reminded them of the anti-Semitic accents of the Slansky trial in 1952. Speakers compared the fate of Israel to that of their country after the Munich agreements of 1938 and denounced the anti-Zionist campaign. On the domestic front, several writers called for an amendment of the law on censorship, freedom of expression and the democratisation of the country. The KSČ leaders rejected and students demonstrated on the streets with the slogan 'We want light! We want to study!' Repression of the demonstrating students by the security forces was brutal, with dozens wounded.[5] Disagreement and resistance of the younger generation to the ruling power was also expressed by means such as the adoption of the long hair, dress style and other aspects of modern Western culture.

In the KSČ, faced with the country's poor economic situation and Novotný's conservatism, some of the party's leaders were in favour of political change. Above all, they wanted economic reform to increase the productivity of the national economy and the standard of living of the population. These reformers also wanted to change the political system and the KSČ itself, but they realised that was impossible while so much power was concentrated in Novotný. In 1967, he was still President of the ČSSR, General Secretary of the KSČ and Supreme Commander of the ČSLA and the People's Militia. In order to carry out reforms, it was necessary at least to deprive him of his position as KSČ General Secretary.

The leader who embodied the reform camp was Aleksander Dubček, the KSS chief who protected both Czech liberals and Slovak autonomists. At the KSČ Central Committee meeting on 30 and 31 October 1967, he took the lead in criticising Novotný's methods. He made a critical appraisal of the state of the country and stressed the need to modify the KSČ programme so that it corresponded to the evolution of society. He also emphasised the national question by highlighting the imbalanced position of Slovakia and its political elites in Czechoslovakia. Above all, he suggested that it was the government that governed, not the Party. He said the KSČ should not replace *de facto* the government. The move against him provoked the wrath of Novotný, who denounced Dubček's "nationalist deviation".[6]

Novotný went to Moscow a few days later for the 50th anniversary of the October Revolution. During his absence, long discussions took place on how to appease the situation. Most Central Committee representatives agreed that Novotný's hold on power had become

Gustav Husák (centre) seen with Erich Honecker (left) and Walter Ulbricht (right) during a visit to East Germany in 1971. (Bundesarchiv)

Due to his critique of the 'old guard' of the KSČ, Aleksander Dubček profiled himself as the leader of the reformist camp and protector of both Czech liberals and Slovak autonomists. In consequence he was elected as the new leader of the KSČ, and the whole of Czechoslovakia, in January 1968. Thus began the Prague Spring.

condemned without compromise the positions taken by the Congress of Writers. This results in exclusions from the KSČ, while the journal of the Union of Writers was placed under the direct authority of the Ministry of Culture.[4]

The intellectuals were not, however, isolated within Czech society, since the students were also moving quickly. The construction of Strahov City University in Prague was celebrated by the regime's propaganda as a success. In reality, many of its buildings had defects, including their power supply. Consequently, on 31 October 1967, untenable. Sensing his position was weakening, the KSČ leader asked for the support of Brezhnev, who arrived in Prague on 8 December.

Surprisingly, the Soviet leader, claiming that he did not want to interfere in the internal affairs of a sister party, did not support either of the opposing factions, only asking that events be resolved quickly and without a political crisis. He nevertheless suggested that Dubček had the confidence of Moscow. This disavowal was a major blow for Novotný, who was a victim of his close relationship with Khrushchev and his coldness towards Brezhnev's rule.[7]

Soviet Prime Minister Alexey Kosygin (left), Soviet leader Leonid Brezhev, and Dubček.

Novotný now relied for his power on the Central Committee's department for the Armed Forces' mobilised generals such as Miroslav Mamula and Jan Šejna, as well as the chiefs of police and the People's Militia. Almost all the elite of the Czechoslovak Army supported him, with the exception of Václav Prchlík and Martin Dzúr. In order to defend Novotný's position, a number of meetings took place. One possible solution was a military intervention aimed at arresting opponents and eliminating all efforts to lead the development of the reform movement.[8] It was in this context that on the morning of 4 December 1967, the 8th Motorised Rifle Regiment of the 13th Tank Division was mobilised in the capital and central and northern Bohemia. However, Generals Dzúr and Prchlík, leaders of the Main Political Administration and Dubček's supporters, carried out a counter-mobilisation.[9] On 11 December, the soldiers were finally demobilised and the 8th Motorised Rifle Regiment sent to the western border of the country until 18 December. In defence of the accusation of having prepared a coup, Defence Minister Bohumír Lomský said that the military manoeuvre was decided well in advance and known to all authorities. To calm the situation, he banned any new military manoeuvre so as not to give the impression of ČSLA interference in the political crisis.

The crisis had to be resolved during the Central Committee meeting at the end of December, where a political battle between three groups took place. The first group, which was still in power and included Novotný's supporters, was in the minority. The second brought together the reformist wing around the economist and government Vice President Ota Šik. The last one brought together the Slovak representatives under the direction of Dubček. Novotný's opponents proposed separating the functions of President of the Republic from those of KSČ General Secretary. While Novotný's position in the Central Committee was still relatively strong, it was nevertheless insufficient to allow him to maintain the leadership of the Party.

Once again, some officers were active, such as Major-General Jan Šejna, who was the most vocal in trying to save Novotný and was ready to stop the entire Central Committee if necessary. He met many times with General Vladimir Janko, Deputy Minister of Defence, who in turn met the commanders of the tank divisions to survey their support.[10] Most of them hesitated and only the commander of the 1st Tank Division was willing to march on Prague, as was General Josef Vosahlo, commander of the Air Force. Generals Šejna and Mamula also visited the ČSLA's commanding officers to push for a petition of support for Novotný. All the generals except Dzúr signed. On 4 January, Šejna assembled all the chiefs of the General Staff to approve a resolution that was effectively an ultimatum to the Central Committee. The following day, at a meeting of the KSČ cell of the

Amid much confusion, elements of the 8th Motorised Rifle Regiment of the 13th Tank Division, ČSLA, were mobilised for deployment to Prague early on 4 December 1967. However, its deployment on the streets – including this OT-62 (a Czechoslovak equivalent of the Soviet-designed BTR-50 armoured personnel carrier), two T-55s, and a column of trucks – was quickly recalled by generals that sided with Dubček and the reformers.

Defence Ministry, he again had his text approved, which he gave to his superior, General Prchlík, head of the ČSLA's main political department, to hand to the Central Committee. However, Prchlík, as a Dubček supporter, kept the resolution in a drawer until the end of the Central Committee meeting.[11]

Novotný managed to retain his position at the head of the KSČ until the Central Committee session which ran from 3–5 January 1968. On the last day of the session, Dubček was finally unanimously elected KSČ General Secretary.[12] The Central Committee also decided to promote a "democratic and developed socialist society in step with the process of democratization".[13] Nevertheless, the fight against Novotný was far from over, since he remained in office as President of the Republic.[14]

The new KSČ leader, and therefore of the country, Dubček, was a moderate and honest communist. He was mostly considered pro-Soviet by Moscow. In the Kremlin, he was called Alexander Stepanovich, and Brezhnev preferred to call him by the affectionate diminutive of Sacha.[15] According to Kuznetsov, former Secretary of the Soviet Embassy in Prague, Dubček seemed to the Soviet leaders "a fairly neutral, weak and insecure person. Always showing great sympathy for the USSR, he made the impression of a politician who would never be opposed to our friendship. He was perceived as a transitory and controllable figure, not as the worst of options."[16] It is also possible that one of the reasons why Brezhnev supported Dubček against Novotný was the latter's refusal to accept the deployment of Soviet troops on Czechoslovak territory, a measure that the dubious Dubček could more easily accede to. However, at a WTO Political Consultative Committee meeting in March 1968, the Soviets realised that the new Czechoslovak leadership also had the same opinion as Novotný on this question.

Although a member of the Central Committee of the KSČ, and then the General Secretary of the party, Dubček was a reform-minded politician: furthermore, dismissal of Novotný quickly made him highly popular with the public.

Restive since 1967, Czechoslovak students were quick in becoming active in support of the reformists within the KSČ.

Spring Reforms

Initially, the Czechoslovak population was very sceptical about the government's change of direction, being convinced that it was only a simple exchange of functions within the KSČ. Yet the dismissal of Novotný made more likely Czechoslovakia's advance on the path to democratisation and reforms. At the end of January, the newspaper *Práce* published an article by the Minister of Forestry, Josef Smrkovský, who claimed to understand that the population was suspicious of the changes that occurred. But according to him, the new leadership was trying to, "make decisions on the basis of democratic principles in the state, the Party and ultimately in all areas".[17]

Faced with Novotný and the many cadres who continued to support him, the reformists needed help, and for that they appealed to public opinion. Since 1948, the media had been a tool for the KSČ and its leaders, but with the gradual abolition of censorship in February and March 1968, freedom of expression became possible.[18] The result was immediate. The accumulated latent dissatisfaction in society, mainly among the intelligentsia, erupted. An open criticism of the style and working methods of the KSČ, trade unions, security apparatus and justice system began. The media also exposed the crimes of the 1950s and failures of the system, and spread the idea of reform in public opinion, thus forming a link between the reformers and the people.[19]

Their main target was Novotný, however: they launched a campaign accusing him of having, in December 1967, envisaged a military intervention against the reformers by using the ČSLA.

The President's position was also weakened when General Šejna, one of his close associates, fled to Hungary and then via Yugoslavia to Italy, before taking refuge in the United States, where he sought political asylum. Šejna had been enriched for years by various trafficking measures, the existence of which was revealed by the media, which also shone a light on his role in the attempted military coup to save Novotný. The scandal was enormous and the position of the President was increasingly fragile. Criticised by political elites, journalists and intellectuals alike, he resigned on 22 March. He was replaced by General Ludvík Svoboda, who was elected on 30 March 1968 by the National Assembly. Novotný was by no means the only one to leave his post, with many resignations following his departure. KSČ officials were dismissed or forced to resign, and the National Assembly President was also replaced.

The reformers took over the direction of the country. On 28 March, the KSČ Central Committee elected Josef Smrkovský as its new President, with Čestmír Císař as Secretary. On 6 April, the government held an extraordinary meeting in which its President, Josef Lenárt, proposed his resignation to President Svoboda. The latter appointed a new government headed by Dubček's relative, Oldřich Černík, who was sworn in on 9 April in the throne room of Prague Castle.[20]

Czechoslovak society, meanwhile, slowly began to boil. The Writers' Union called for the rehabilitation of "citizens illegally sentenced in the past", while the Czechoslovak Youth Union wanted to become independent of the KSČ and the Slovak National Council called for the creation of a federal state. Organisations were formed to defend their interests, such as the Club of Committed Non-Party Members (Klub angazovanych nestraniku, or KAN), founded on 5 April, and Club 231, created on 31 March to bring together victims of Stalinist repression.[21] To some, these groups appeared to be embryos of political parties. Vaclav Havel even called for the formation of an opposition party, and the philosopher Ivan Svitak supported a multi-party political system.[22] Such moves did not seem unrealistic, as the Social Democrats were starting to organise themselves to form a party that could appear as a political alternative to the communists.

Action Programme

The KSČ Central Committee, which met in March and April at Prague Castle, seemed to be in keeping with popular aspirations. It sought the rehabilitation of those unjustly condemned in the 1950s and cancelled the exclusion of the writers Ludvík Vaculík, Ivan Klíma and Antonín Liebm, who were punished after the Fourth Congress of Writers, while the disciplinary proceedings against Milan Kundera were stopped. It also decided to modify the role of the government so that it really only exercised its constitutional function and responsibility before the National Assembly, to guarantee and defend the rights and liberties of the citizens and ensure the development of the national economy. On 1 April 1968, it approved what was known as the Action Programme, which was published on 9 April.

The Action Programme, which became one of the central documents of the Prague Spring, aimed to address the problems and mistakes of the past based on a critical analysis of the 1950s and 1960s. The core of the programme was the promotion of a socialist democracy so that Czechoslovakia would embark on its own socialist path while maintaining its alliance with the Soviet Union and other communist countries. The document insisted on the notions of sovereignty, mutual respect and international solidarity, and indicated that Prague "will specify its own point of view on the fundamental questions of world politics".[23]

The KSČ did not give up its leading role but rejected the form of totalitarian power established in 1948. It advocated a clear separation of powers between the Party and the government. The latter had to be more accountable to the parliament, which had to be more representative by integrating more representatives of non-communist parties. Dubček also promised to guarantee the right to travel abroad, to rehabilitate the victims of the purges, and to purge and reorganise State Security. He also planned to decentralise and rebalance the economy, normalise relations with the Church and establish a federal state structure based on equality between Czechs and Slovaks.[24] The implementation of this programme, which aimed to establish "a socialism with a human face", was entrusted to the government led by Černík.

Unlike the Hungarian reformers of 1956, Czechoslovak leaders favoured a revolution from above in order to avoid the tragic repetition of the Budapest uprising. To this end, special emphasis had been placed on gradual and evolving changes in political institutions to ensure the stability of the country and the irreversibility of change. Their goal was not to destroy socialism, but to make it better and more beneficial. This should therefore not result in a change of regime, but rather in a correction of the deficiencies and errors of the existing system.

In the economic field, Šik, the new Minister of Economy and Deputy Prime Minister, decided to evaluate the work of industrial enterprises not according to the degree of realisation of the plan, but on the basis of the demand of their products in domestic and foreign markets. Dubček also supported the idea of eliminating inefficient and obsolete enterprises, stating that Czechoslovak factories were still far from being able to meet real demand and that the structure of the economy was imperfect, because it departed from the principles that determined developed industrialised countries. Yet this was not a desire to return to a market economy, since the reform provided for the creation of worker councils integrating a larger share and influence of the workers on the operation of the company. Small private enterprises had to be authorised, and cooperation with foreign companies was also considered.[25]

Faced with this programme, Novotný's supporters hit back, denouncing the rise of "anti-socialist forces" in the country and the collapse of Party authority. They could count on the support of thousands of Party and state apparatus cadres who feared losing their privileges. There was also a gradual change in the Party leadership, involving some members toward the so-called conservative wing. A dynamic polarisation process thus began.[26] The conservatives placed their hopes in the Soviets, who, according to them, would not tolerate such liberalism at a time when a neo-Stalinism was prevailing in the USSR. Importantly, they still had an important influence in the National Assembly and the Central Committee. For Dubček's supporters, there was no hope of completing their reformist programme without renewing the governing body, which was only possible by convening a KSČ Congress in advance. This congress had three objectives: to write a federal law, elect a new Central Committee and integrate the programme of reforms into the KSČ statutes.[27]

At the end of May, the Central Committee met in a tense atmosphere between conservatives and liberals. Dubček reassured his opponents, stressing that the leading role of the Party could not be questioned and that no opposition party would be allowed. The Central Committee decided to convene an extraordinary KSČ Congress on 9 September. Dubček hoped this congress would make it possible to get rid of

The polarisation between conservatives and liberals within the top levels of the KSČ resulted in proponents of either wing openly agitating for one wing and against another in the streets of Czechoslovak cities.

Novotný's supporters, but also the radical reformers who endangered the leading role of the KSČ and fuelled the fears of Moscow.[28]

The convocation of the congress provoked an effervescence in the country, since it was now up to 1,700,000 KSČ militants to settle the conflict between the liberals and the conservatives. Election fever was intense, as it was the delegates elected by the local party organisations who would determine the future of the country by electing a new leadership and approving its programme. Meanwhile, the wind of reform which blew across Czechoslovakia did not spare the ČSLA.

ČSLA and the Prague Spring

Throughout the 1960s, in order to comply with the Warsaw Pact's strategic guidelines, the ČSLA had undergone many transformations that resulted in reorganisations, the creation and dissolution of various types of units and the continuous modernisation of weapons and equipment in a context of lack of matériel and human resources, with the requirements imposed exceeding the capacity of the state to respect them. These perpetual changes caused dissatisfaction among the military. Economic problems also led to the adoption of austerity measures that affected the material situation of professional soldiers. Their families faced problems with housing shortages and access to health care, cultural and sports facilities, while many barracks were dilapidated.[29]

The coming to power of Dubček and the reformers caused many upheavals within the ČSLA. At the end of March 1968, the National Assembly convened a Military and Security Committee, the first step to ensure that the Army was no longer exclusively managed by the KSČ. The changes in the Armed Forces leadership in early 1968, with the replacement on 8 April of Bohumír Lomský as Defence Minister by Martin Dzúr, or that of the CoS, General Rytir, by Karel Rusov on 30 April, disorganised the ČSLA command, which was divided between 'progressives' and 'conservatives'. The crisis in the ČSLA was aggravated by the suspension of training at the battalion level for five months following suspicions about the use of the Army in favour of Novotný. To make matters worse, a new reorganisation of ČSLA units had begun as part of the federalisation of the state. Changes were made to the location of units: some were to go to Slovakia and others to the Czech part of the country.[30]

The ČSLA experienced a decline in discipline as KSČ groups lost their position in the ranks of the Army. Using the model of what happened in the rest of society, associations of professional soldiers began to form spontaneously to defend the interests of the military, such as the Czechoslovakian Air Force Association. A number of radical demands emerged, including calls for the establishment of democratically elected bodies at all levels of command, maximum independence from the KSČ and the introduction of non-communist political movements in the Armed Forces.[31] The rehabilitation of servicemen who had been victims of repression in the 1950s was also requested, and a commission of rehabilitation was created on 30 April. Questions about conscripts, professional soldiers and civilian employees were discussed at a Military Youth Forum in Znojmo in early May. ČSLA leaders also had to make specific changes, such as soldiers' leave, their right to wear civilian clothes off-duty and reduced prices on trains and buses for soldiers.[32]

The military leaders also did not hesitate to express their criticism of the ČSLA's management, complaining on 25 March during a Military Council that since 1960, the government had, at the request of the Soviets, reduced the budget of the Army but without reducing its numbers. General Vosáhl asked for conscripts to be given hot water and social clubs, while professional soldiers needed improved legal status and career prospects, and better management and housing services.[33]

Most importantly, however, the government's management of the ČSLA under parliamentary control was reflected in the definition of a new Czechoslovak military doctrine. These issues were addressed in the May Memorandum drafted by a team of scientists from the Klement Gottwald Politico-Military Academy in Prague. This memo defined a new military doctrine that considered both "the national interest" and "the interest of the main coalition state", i.e. the USSR, to favour a defensive strategy rather than "the wrong choice of the offensive strategy". In the opinion of the Memorandum's authors, a nuclear war in Europe would inevitably mean the destruction of the country. They therefore advocated a limited war without the use of nuclear weapons. Above all, they believed that a war in Europe could only be the result of the inability to conclude a peace treaty with the FRG and to resolve the West Berlin problem. In order to improve the international situation, the May Memorandum therefore proposed to conclude international agreements with Austria, France and the FRG on the basis of mutual renunciation of the threat of violence.[34] Such a doctrine, that called into question Soviet strategy, would become a nightmare for Moscow.

The Action Programme of the ČSLA on 21 May 1968, drafted by the KSČ Military-Administrative Department headed by General Prchlík, was less radical, but it still criticised the state of defence of

A Praga V3S truck of the ČSLA in early 1968. This was a highly-reliable, and popular, multi-purpose vehicle manufactured from 1953 until 1964, that was also widely exported.

the country because of the unconditional alignment to Soviet policy, the unjustified cost of maintaining the ČSLA in the Warsaw Pact and the unequal relations that existed within the alliance. It nonetheless advocated the maintenance of the country in the Warsaw Pact, but called for an improvement in the functioning of the alliance through the creation of a Military Staff Council and a more elaborate Joint Command.[35]

Far from being a purely civilian affair, the Prague Spring did not spare the ČSLA either at the level of its organisation or its military doctrine. Here again, as in the rest of society, the desire to abandon the shackles that had surrounded Czechoslovakia since 1948 was expressed. This aspiration, which was reflected in multiple free debates, speeches and appeals, provoked tensions. Some people advocated a radicalisation of the reform movement, while others were worried about a possible questioning of the political and ideological foundations of the regime.

The 'Two Thousand Words'

The conservatives, who could not prevent the convocation of the KSČ Congress, mobilised their supporters in the administration, the Party apparatus and the People's Militia. At the Central Committee meeting on 29 May and 1 June, conservatives criticised economic reforms and warned of social pressures on the Party apparatus. Dubček's supporters remained in the majority, but the leadership was more cautious about the pace of reforms. In response, the liberals were far from inactive. On 27 June, *Literarni Listy*, the Writers' Union Journal, published what was known as the 'Two Thousand Words' manifesto.[36] This text, addressed to the communists and the population as a whole, was a harsh criticism of those who had ruled the country. To prevent their return, they called for a mobilisation of the population through public meetings, demonstrations and strikes. The signatories of the text also announced that they were ready to defend by arms the government if it pursued its liberalisation policy, a barely veiled allusion to the risk of a foreign intervention to stop the Prague Spring. The 'Two Thousand Words' provoked the wrath of the Kremlin. *Pravda* of 11 July wrote that the text was "the platform of forces that, in Czechoslovakia and beyond its borders, under cover of gossip about liberalisation, democratisation, etc., are trying to draw a line through the whole history of Czechoslovakia since 1948 ... to discredit the Czechoslovak party, to deny its leading role."[37]

The 'Two Thousand Words', while a challenge, was also a symptom of the inability of the radical reformers to perceive the real international situation and the resulting possibilities for change. It was especially a weapon for the conservatives and their supporters in Moscow, who found in it an argument to denounce a plot to destroy the power of the KSČ and restore capitalism in Czechoslovakia. In Czech society, its radical tone provoked conflicting responses, from enthusiastic consent to categorical rejection, while Western observers called it a declaration of useless irritation to Moscow and a tactical error.[38]

Dubček and Černík also denounced the text but refused to take sanctions against the authors when the conservatives tried to mobilise the workers against the "anti-socialist" intellectuals. The majority of the population supported Dubček's liberal programme and was united in defending the sovereignty of the Party and the nation. This national unanimity forced the conservative opposition into silence. Above all, there was nothing anti-communist in the support for Dubček, and people still trusted the KSČ. Nor was it anti-Soviet. Indeed, in total, only a few Czechoslovaks had pushed for the country to opt for neutrality: their leadership was aware that it was impossible to change the balance of power in Europe without triggering a war. They also had in mind the Hungarian events of 1956 and were aware that they could not cross certain limits without provoking Soviet anger. They began to take action against a possible anti-socialist insurrection, marginalised the Social Democrats and framed the freedom of the press.[39]

The absence of hostility towards the USSR and the refusal to leave the WTO or change the social system gave hope to the Czechoslovak leaders that the Kremlin would let Dubček consolidate the regime by reforming it. Yet, despite these assurances, the Prague Spring was quickly deemed unacceptable by the Soviets and labelled a danger to the socialist system.

4
THE FIVE AGAINST PRAGUE

The transformations that affected Czechoslovakia after Dubček's assumption of power were not without consequences in the rest of the socialist world. The latter was not a monolith, and the countries that composed it had a certain margin of manoeuvre, as shown by the reforms carried out in Hungary after 1956 or Nicolae Ceausescu's policy in Romania. This autonomy was framed and subordinated to two imperatives however: maintaining the absolute hegemony of the Communist Party and keeping the country within the Warsaw Pact. Nevertheless, the development of the Prague Spring raised fears in Moscow and the capitals of the other Eastern Bloc countries that the Czechs were crossing these boundaries and moving away from the Soviet fold.

The rise of tensions

The arrival of a reformer like Dubček at the head of the KSČ could only worry Moscow, despite the assurances that he gave to Brezhnev when they met in Moscow on 29 January 1968.[1] For all Soviet leaders, the only possible and correct model of socialism remained that defined by the Kremlin, and every deviation from the official policy of the USSR was considered a threat to the very nature of socialism. With the arrival of Brezhnev in power in 1964, a return to Stalinism began, a path totally contrary to that taken in early 1968 by Czechoslovakia, which was moving away from Stalinist stagnation to adopt a democratic concept of socialism.

Brezhnev nevertheless trusted Dubček when he went to Prague on 21 and 22 February. He understood the need to carry out reforms to help Czechoslovakia out of stagnation – especially economic stagnation – and believed that Dubček was able to lead them without undermining the foundations of the ČSSR. This demonstrative support was supposed to influence the position of the leaders of the other socialist countries, in particular Poland's Wladyslaw Gomułka and East Germany's Walter Ulbricht, who were particularly critical of the policies of the Czechoslovak leadership.[2] At the meeting of the WTO Political Consultative Committee on 6 and 7 March in Sofia, the Czechoslovak question was not discussed openly, although Ulbricht and Gomułka repeatedly tried to push Brezhnev to do so.

Brezhnev's position evolved, however, because of the information he received from Czechoslovakia. On this point, the role of the Soviet ambassador in Prague,[3] Stepan Chervonenko, was crucial. He was an ambassador of great experience and his opinion had authority in Moscow. He had previously been ambassador to Beijing at the time of the Sino–Soviet split, and feared that if he lost control of events in Czechoslovakia, he would be accused of losing another country.[4] As a result, he was very hostile to Dubček and from March onwards he warned about the possibility of a "second Hungary". Chervonenko's reports presented Dubček as enjoying the sympathy of a "small handful of intellectuals" and completely deprived of the support of the masses, especially among the workers. According to the ambassador, they remained supporters of the USSR, but a handful of right-wingers prevented them from expressing their opinion.[5] In addition to Soviet diplomats, one of the main sources of information for the Soviet leadership was the reports of representatives of the 'pro-Soviet' group in Czechoslovakia. Knowing the Kremlin's fears, their information gave the impression that Czechoslovak reforms threatened the vital interests of the Soviet Union in Eastern Europe.

János Kádár, General Secretary of the Hungarian Socialist Workers' Party and President of Hungary from 1956 until 1988. While initially given the role of an intermediary between Prague and Moscow, subsequently he was to become one of the fiercest proponents of the WTO's military intervention.

The situation in Czechoslovakia was therefore rapidly becoming one of the main topics of discussion at the CPSU Political Bureau meetings. Brezhnev criticised Dubček first of all for the movement of personnel within the KSČ. This had excluded Party secretaries, department heads of the Central Committee and faithful ministers of Novotný, despite the promises made to the Kremlin and without the candidates chosen to replace them being accepted by Moscow. For Brezhnev, such "disrespect" was the first alarming sign that Dubček was moving away from the "collective line of the socialist community".[6]

The end of censorship in Prague was a new reason for dissatisfaction. At the Politburo meeting of 15 March, Boris Ponomarev, chief of the International Department of the CPSU Central Committee, proposed to write a letter to the KSČ denouncing Czechoslovak journalists who wanted to detach their country from the socialist camp and the Soviet Union. Yuri Andropov, leader of the KGB – and who would go on to succeed Brezhnev following his death in 1982 – was more menacing, comparing the evolution of Czechoslovakia to that of Hungary in 1956.[7] Brezhnev was much more cautious and met Dubček in Prague to discuss the situation. The latter once again reassured the Soviet leader, and the two men agreed on a meeting between Dubček and Hungarian leader Janos Kádár, who would play a mediating role.

A few days later, Dubček duly met Kádár, who warned him of a possible evolution comparable to that of his country in 1956. The Hungarian leader knew that Prague was isolated within the WTO. The Poles and East Germans were indeed suspicious of the situation in Czechoslovakia, fearing a contagion of the Prague model that could call into question their own power. It was with the Poles that relations were most strained. In Poland, a student protest following the banning of a play was severely repressed. Warsaw took the opportunity to launch a purge in the media, the universities and the Party apparatus that targeted liberal communists of Jewish origin accused of Zionism. Faced with these events, the students and intellectuals of Bratislava and Prague showed their solidarity with the victims of repression in Poland, which led to a cooling of relations between the two countries.

The meeting of the CPSU Politburo on 21 March marked a hardening of the Soviets' position. Aleksei Kosygin said Czechoslovakia actually took the path to Hungary in 1956, while Mikhail Solomentsev emphasised the relationship between events in Prague and the development of the opposition movement in the USSR. Brezhnev again tried to reassure them by pointing out that Dubček had assured him that order would be maintained and that he would continue to maintain a friendly relationship with Moscow.[8]

The Kremlin's main preoccupation was the emergence of opposition groups such as KAN and Club 231, which were in fact only at an embryonic stage and gathered few supporters. The CPSU was also concerned about the prospect of legalisation of the Social Democratic Party and growing criticism of Moscow in the Czechoslovak media. Furthermore, the Kremlin was under pressure from some Warsaw Pact countries, which were increasingly hostile to the Czechoslovak experience. In March, the GDR was the first country to declare the situation in Prague was counter-revolutionary.[9] Zhivkov, the leader of Bulgaria, during a meeting with Brezhnev in Sofia in early March, declared he was ready to use his armed forces against the Czechs. The idea was resumed at the CPSU Politburo, where Kirill Mazurov warned that the WTO had to prepared for the worst.[10]

On 23 March, a meeting of the leaders of the Warsaw Pact – with the exception of those of Romania – was held in Dresden. Czechoslovakia was represented by Dubček, Josef Lenárt, Černík, Drahomir Kolder and Vasil Biľak. Economic questions were due to be the main agenda of the meeting, but shortly after their arrival, the Czechoslovak representatives were informed that the discussion would only concern the situation in their country. Speeches made by Ulbricht, Kádár, Kosygin, Brezhnev and Gomułka expressed

'Where's that counterrevolution' – a big poster of the kind that would appear in many places around Czechoslovakia once the WTO intervention began. Ironically, not one of the leaders of the – supposedly – allied countries that had ordered the intervention – could provide a clear answer.

A group-photo following the WTO-meeting in Dresden in March 1968, showing (centre, from left to right) Aleksey Kosygin, Nikolay Podgorny, Walter Ulbricht and Aleksandar Dubček. Visible behind Kosygin and Podgorny is the Hungarian leader Kádár, one of strongest proponents of the WTO intervention.

strong concern at the evolution of the situation in Czechoslovakia. According to them, the reform process meant the coming to power of anti-socialist and anti-Soviet forces, the development of a counter-revolution and the loss of leadership of the country by the KSČ. They also feared that the country would withdraw from the WTO, and it was therefore necessary to end this process swiftly and forcefully.[11] Dubček, surprised by the ferocity of the attacks, responded with an improvised speech promising to regain control of the media. He also asked that no official release be published from the meeting openly criticizing Czechoslovakia's leaders.[12]

Upon his return to Prague, Dubček declared himself to be reassured. He said:

Our friends want the success of our work and have assured us of their full support. It is natural for them to worry about the danger of anti-socialist elements taking advantage of our democratization process. We provided them with detailed explanations, which greatly helped them to understand the KSČ central committee's policy.[13]

However, condemnation of the Czechoslovak reformers was not unanimous. Some of the participants at the Dresden meeting, in particular Kádár, remained more cautious in their attacks on Dubček's policy. On 18 April, the Hungarian leader even cautiously expressed his agreement on a number of KSČ measures. The Dresden meeting therefore appeared as a warning to Prague: the KSČ needed to better control the situation and avoid the loss of its monopoly of power. Brezhnev always trusted Dubček and believed him capable of controlling the situation in his country. The election of General Svoboda as President was also welcomed, the latter having the confidence of Moscow, including the Soviet military.

Critics of the Prague Spring could not blame the KSČ for challenging the Marxist doctrine, nor the inviolability of the alliance with the USSR or their obligations in the WTO. The Czechoslovaks remained in the framework of the principles of the 'socialist community' defined by Moscow, which prevented a definitive condemnation of their policy by the USSR and the other Warsaw Pact countries. While the Chinese and Albanians were very hostile towards Prague, Yugoslavia and Romania showed sympathy, whereas *Pravda* took a neutral stance. Hungarian Prime Minister Jenő Fock, during a speech on Budapest radio on 20 April, even claimed the situation in Czechoslovakia was an internal affair in that country, and the Bulgarian leader, Zhivkov, arrived in Prague on 23 April to sign a 'Treaty of friendship and cooperation'.[14]

The KSČ Action Programme and the articles in the Czech press demanding the KSČ expel from its ranks those who were involved in the repression of the 1950s were still problematic to the Soviets. Their implementation could indeed lead to the explosion of the country's political system, directly threatening almost all the representatives of the Party and state elite. Ulbricht, still the most fervent opponent of the Czechoslovak reforms, denounced the Action Programme, while Brezhnev seemed to agree with him at the CPSU Central Committee from 6–10 April, when he called it a "revisionist" text. Gomułka, meanwhile, asked the Soviet military to consider the occupation of Czechoslovakia by Warsaw Pact forces.[15]

The military option

Following the Dresden meeting, Soviet leaders began to think of military measures against Czechoslovakia. The adoption of the Action Programme appeared to be proof that the warnings given in Dresden had not been heard by Prague. But at this point, the use of force was still only one option among others, and it appeared the least credible. Nevertheless, the Soviet military were preparing themselves to be ready in case there were no other alternatives.

On 8 April, Marshal Andrei Grechko, Soviet Defence Minister, signed a top-secret directive to launch preparations for an invasion of Czechoslovakia. It was addressed to the Soviet troops deployed in the Warsaw Pact countries and in the USSR:

- the GSFG in the GDR under the command of Army General Pyotr Koshevoy,
- the Northern Group of Forces stationed in Poland under the command of General Ivan Shkadov,
- the Southern Group of Forces in Hungary under the command of General Konstantin Provalov,
- the Carpathian Military District under the command of General Vasily Bisyarin,
- the command of the Airborne troops under General Vasily Margelov,
- the command of the Air Force led by Marshal Konstantin Vershinin,
- the command of the Missile Forces under Marshal Nikolai Krylov,
- the command of the Air Defence led by Marshal Batice,
- the Naval command of Admiral Sergey Gorshkov.[16]

The development of the invasion plan, which was to be called Operation Danube, was entrusted to General Mikhail Povaliy, head of the Defence Council of the USSR and the Planning Chief of the Soviet General Staff. It was first conceived as a military exercise which had to justify the transfer and concentration of troops. Its objective was clear:

As early as of April 1968, the Soviet political and military leadership began planning a military intervention in Czechoslovakia. These young recruits operating an IS-3 heavy tank of the Soviet Army, were soon to re-deploy from their base in the western USSR in that direction.

One rarely seen vehicle that participated in Operation Danube was the SU-122-54 – a self-propelled gun on the chassis of T-54 tank (see colour section for details).

The counter-revolutionary forces in Czechoslovakia supported by the United States and the FRG broke the order in that country. In order to exploit these events, NATO troops invade Czechoslovakia, overthrow popular government and establish a friendly regime [...] The Soviet Union and other socialist countries, faithful to their international commitment and to the Warsaw Pact, are obliged to bring their troops to the aid of the Czechoslovak People's Army for the defence of their homeland against this threat.[17]

A few days later, on 12 April, the commander of the 38th Army of the Carpathian Military District, General Mayorov was urgently summoned to the District Commander, General Bisyarin. He presented him with a map dated 11 April which indicated the operation area of his army in Czechoslovakia. For this operation, Mayorov directed the 24th, 30th, 48th and 128th Motorised Rifle Divisions, 15th and 31st Tank Divisions and the 12th Motorised Rifle Regiment of the Bulgarian People's Army. Its goal was to reach the Moravská Ostrava–Brno line, a distance of 500–550km, in 24 hours. According to Povaliy, the map and accompanying instructions were personally approved by Brezhnev. He was asked to keep the operation absolutely secret, since only the commanders of military districts and groups of troops abroad, the members of the Military Council, and the commanders of the armies participating in the invasion knew the existence of this plan.[18] Less than three months after Dubček's accession to power, the outline of Operation Danube had already been established.

For this operation, Moscow – considering the lessons learned from the Hungarian events of 1956 and in order to avoid international complications – decided to act within the framework of the WTO. On 19 and 23 April, Deputy Defence Minister and WTO C-in-C Ivan Yakubovsky visited the GDR, Poland and Bulgaria to request the participation of the armed forces of these countries in Operation Danube. The agreement of the Poles was obtained on 19 April after an interview with Gomułka. Polish general Florian Sawicky rapidly participated in the preparations for invasion.[19] Preparations for Operation Danube, while remaining secret and only appearing in the form of a military exercise, paved the way for a military solution to the Czechoslovak crisis.

Pressure on Prague

Although Brezhnev felt the military option should only be used as a last resort, he had to take into consideration the hawks who surrounded him, such as Grechko, Andropov, Mikhail Suslov or Petro Shelest.[20] They did not trust Dubček, and the appearance of political clubs, the resurgence of the Social Democratic Party and media criticism of socialist Czechoslovakia's past were seen as a sign that the KSČ was gradually losing control of the situation, a prelude to a definitive loss of power. If this prospect was unbearable for the Kremlin, it was even more so for the other WTO countries. Their position had a considerable influence on the balance within the Soviet leadership between the moderates and those in favour of an uncompromising stance towards Prague. A special note from the International Department of the CPSU Central Committee indicated that the leaders of the GDR, Poland, Bulgaria and, to a lesser extent, Hungary "consider the Czechoslovak events as a direct threat to their regimes, a dangerous infection that can spread in their countries".[21] In an interview with Soviet officials, the GDR leadership expressed their opinions "on the advisability of providing collective assistance to the fraternal leadership of Czechoslovakia, going as far as the use of extreme measures".[22] Zhivkov took a similar position. After visiting Prague at the end of April, he informed Moscow that he believed the counter-revolution was unfolding more and more in Czechoslovakia and that capitalism was ready to be reinstated.[23] Only the Hungarian leaders remained more cautious, but nevertheless considered that the situation in Czechoslovakia seemed the "prologue to the counter-revolutionary insurrection in Hungary" of 1956.[24]

On 4 May, Dubček, Černík, Smrkovský and Biľak (a member of the Presidium of the KSČ) arrived in Moscow to meet Brezhnev, Kosygin, Nikolai Podgorny (chairman of the Presidium of the Supreme Soviet), Konstantin, and Katushev (members of the Secretariat of the CPSU Central Committee). The meeting was held at the request of Czechoslovak representatives wishing to discuss economic issues, including a loan application. However, Moscow's concerns weren't economic. Again, Czechoslovakia was subjected to severe criticism. Brezhnev denounced the Action Programme as opening the possibility of the restoration of capitalism in Czechoslovakia. He indicated that he was concerned about the evolution of the situation and asked how the CPSU could help.[25] During the discussions, Černík admitted that since the April Central Committee, the situation had become serious and anti-socialist forces were trying to discredit the KSČ. Brezhnev believed there was an organised process in Czechoslovakia against the KSČ, and, as a threat, recalled the Hungarian experience. Dubček also now considered the situation to be serious and said he would take urgent measures to consolidate the situation.[26]

On 6 May, Brezhnev, after meeting with the Prague leaders, opened a meeting of the CPSU Politburo with the aim of finding the best options for resolving the Czechoslovak issue. He again condemned the Action Programme and declared it an unacceptable move away from socialism. He decided to increase pressure on Prague's leaders

From left to right: Černík, Dubček, Svoboda and Smrkovský, during a break in one of many meetings in the spring of 1968.

by carrying out a WTO military exercise on Czechoslovak territory and close to its borders, with the participation of GSFG troops and perhaps even those of Poland. This exercise was a warning to the Prague reformers to redress the situation and keep the promises they had made to him.[27]

On 8 May, Brezhnev again informed the leaders of the GDR, Poland, Bulgaria and Hungary, in response to requests for military intervention by Ulbricht, Zhivkov and Gomułka, that it was still not necessary to engage in military action against Czechoslovakia.[28] He set out the solution he proposed two days earlier before the Politburo to launch a WTO military exercise on Czechoslovak territory. All participants agreed this exercise should be held as soon as possible, with the troops remaining in Czechoslovakia for as long as possible.[29]

Exercise Šumava

Until now, what became known as Exercise Šumava did not have a clearly defined date. Yakubovsky therefore went to the GDR, Poland and Bulgaria from 19–23 April, to Czechoslovakia on 24 and 25 April and to Hungary on 27 April to demand that the military exercise take place in Czechoslovak territory. In Warsaw, on 19 April, he met Gomułka, Prime Minister Józef Cyrankiewicz, Defence Minister General Jaruzelski and the CoS. The Poles, who were strong supporters of the implementation of such an exercise, agreed and designated the Second Polish Army of the Silesian Military District to participate in it.[30]

For Yakubovsky the most difficult thing to do when he arrived in Prague on 24 April was to convince the Czechs that the exercise could be held on their territory in May. The Defence Minister, General Dzúr, rejected the proposal and suggested to the KSČ Central Committee that the exercise not be held that year. However, a resolution of the KSČ on 30 April ordered the acceleration of preparations to carry it out, without setting a specific date for its start.[31] This Prague concession certainly aimed to reassure Moscow and show its loyalty to the WTO at a time when, according to a statement by Biľak in April 1990, Soviet leaders suggested that Czechoslovakia agree to a Soviet division being stationed on its territory to protect the western border, a request that the Czechs had refused.[32]

The Soviet request to transfer troops to Czechoslovak territory was accompanied by troop movements. On 5 May, General Mayorov received an encrypted telegram from the General Staff instructing him to place his troops in preparation for combat and to deploy them, on the morning of 7 May, 7km northeast of Uzhhorod. The 128th Motorised Rifle Division was to be installed in the region of Mukachevo in western Ukraine. On 5 May, General Grigory Yashkin, commanding the 24th Motorised Rifle Division, was ordered to move his division to Poland, and then on 9 May to the Czechoslovak border. According to Yakubovsky's orders, the division was to cross the border at 1100 hours and advance to the western Czechoslovak border. However, a dozen Czechoslovak T34/85 tanks were reported nearby, and Yakubovsky finally cancelled the order.[33] This particular

Marshal Ivan Yakubovsky, Commander-in-Chief of the General Staff, Soviet Armed Forces and the Warsaw Pact forces (right), meeting the East German leader Ulbrich.

The crews of Polish T-55s clean the 100mm main guns of their vehicles in spring 1968.

Through May 1968, multiple units of the Soviet Army converged on the borders to Czechoslovakia, always under the guise of running joint exercises with neighbouring armed forces. This photograph shows a participating T-62 main battle tank.

episode of the Czechoslovakian crisis was undoubtedly linked to the belief in Moscow that Prague would allow its troops to be installed on its territory, as Yakubovsky apparently asked during his trip to Czechoslovakia. The Czech refusal would have led to the final cancellation of the operation.

Movements of troops on the Czechoslovak border, however, continued during the following days. From 11–15 May, the Polish 10th and 11th Tank Divisions and the Soviet 24th Motorised Rifle Division took part in a joint exercise.[34] The presence of a Soviet division on the Czechoslovak border with the GDR was masked by a bilateral exercise from 10–17 May which involved a tank army of the GSFG and two divisions of the East German NVA – about 60 000 soldiers and 1,800 tanks.[35]

On 13 May, the CPSU Central Committee sent a note to Grechko and Yakubovsky to set a date for the start of Exercise Šumava.[36] On 17 May, the head of the Soviet government, Kosygin, arrived in Czechoslovakia, preceded by a military delegation led by Grechko. The Soviets wanted to allay Czech fears. The day after their arrival, a member of the delegation, General Epishev, refuted in a television interview the rumours of a possible Soviet intervention, describing them as "a crude and stupid fiction".[37] On 22 May, Kosygin himself spoke on Czechoslovak television to declare he considered "the Czechs and Slovaks as our great friends and that is quite understandable because we have come a long way together and our Parties are fighting on the same front".[38]

Discussions between the Soviet and Czechoslovak military continued until 22 May. The ČSLA leaders faced Soviet criticism and a refusal to provide them with KRUG (SA-4 Ganef) and KUB (SA-6 Gainful) or S-125 (SA-3 GOA) air defence equipment. Nevertheless, the Soviets finally managed to get the date of Exercise Šumava set for 20–30 June.[39] The commanders and staffs of all WTO troops were to participate in this exercise. The intention was to "prepare the forces and the command of the troops under the conditions of modern operations and to increase the combat readiness of the troops and their staffs".[40]

On 23 May, Grechko reported to the CPSU Politburo the results of the military delegation's trip. According to him, the ČSLA was in a state of total decomposition, with orders no longer executed, while the forces stationed on the FRG border had only 40–50 percent of their normal strength. On 27 May, Kosygin reported to the Politburo on the results of his visit to Prague. It was reassuring. The Czechoslovakian leaders had assured him that "if the events take place in a brutal manner and this cannot be ruled out, they see a solution in the use of the People's Militia".[41] Nevertheless, Brezhnev confirmed the decision to exert pressure on Prague by launching Exercise Šumava.

Show of Force

While primarily a means of applying pressure on Prague, Exercise Šumava was also a test for military intervention. Immediately after the end of negotiations over its start date, preparations for the exercise began; from 24–26 May, the training areas of the ČSLA, airports, border crossing points, routes of the participating units as well as the places of their installation were all inspected.[42] The Soviets visited air bases that were to host the exercises involving the following air units: a MiG-21 squadron at Zatec, two others at Hradcany, two Sukhoi Su-7 squadrons at Caslav, a MiG-19 squadron at Hradec Králové, a Jak-28R reconnaissance squadron at Pardubice and a Mi-4 helicopter squadron at Kbely airport. Mlada, headquarters of the exercise command, was

A MiG-21R, of the Soviet air force, participating in Exercise Šumava. Barely visible underneath the drop tank is a D-Type pod, equipped with reconnaissance cameras.

Soviet airborne troops undergoing inspection prior to embarkation aboard Antonov An-12 transports.

Soviet airborne troops loading their ASU-57 assault gun onto a pallet on which it is going to be para-dropped over the jump zone. The vehicle was designed for transport by An-12 aircraft (one of which is visible in the background), and could be air-dropped from it with help of the rocket-assisted parachute (for details on the ASU-57, see the colour section).

to receive 16 Mi-4 helicopters, one Ilyushin IL-14 transport aircraft and two Lisunov Li-2 aircraft. Faced with the refusal of the Czechoslovakians to such an air deployment in their country, the only aircraft to eventually participate were 18 Mi-4s, two Li-2s, an IL-14, an IL-18, a Soviet An-24 and a Polish IL-14 at Mlada, 10 MiG-21s and a Soviet MiG-21UTI at Hradčany airport, 10 Su-7BMs, 10 MiG-17s, and two Soviet MiG-15UTIs at Čáslav, and nine Yak-28Rs and a Yak-28RU at Pardubic airport.[43]

Soviet officers also took advantage of preparations for the exercise to collect information on the capacity of bridges or airports and to build a large communication network of radio and telephone-cables. The intelligence component of Exercise Šumava would also gauge the state of mind of the Czechoslovakian population and the ČSLA, and monitor the Czechoslovak Army's combat capabilities, including its ability to provide organised resistance in case of WTO troops' entry into the country.

Initially, the exercise was to mobilise around 14,000 Warsaw Pact soldiers. But little by little, from 28 May and particularly after 30 May, the Soviets began increasing the number of units involved in the exercise, expanding the scope of their activities and then bringing as many troops as possible to Czechoslovakia from neighbouring states. A total of 23,721 soldiers, 6,344 vehicles, 79 tanks and 87 aircraft and helicopters participated in the exercise on Czech territory.[44] The total number of troops simultaneously involved in exercises in the GDR, Poland, the USSR and Hungary was estimated at between 30,000 and 40,000.[45] Faced with this unprecedented deployment of forces, Czechoslovak officials soon realised that the real objectives of the exercise were not those stated at the outset.

The Czechoslovakian military especially noticed that the duration of Šumava was stretched. The previous similar exercise, Exercise Vltava of September 1966, had been planned, prepared and repeated in nine months. Analysis had taken place the day after it was completed, and the Soviet troops had withdrawn in just four days. Exercise Šumava was to be finished on 30 June and evaluated the next day. Marshal Yakubovsky considered the state of combat training of the ČSLA insufficient and proposed to continue the exercise, without indicating a date for its completion.[46] There were rumours among the population that the Soviets intended to stay until the 14th KSČ Congress in September. On 1 July, Czechoslovak officials wrote to Brezhnev asking that he end the exercise and withdraw the WTO troops.[47] The next day, a full evaluation of the exercise was finally completed.

The Czechoslovak leadership, by constant insistence, appeared to have achieved its goal, but matters were not so clear-cut. After the end of the exercise, although the Hungarian troops returned to their barracks and the ČSLA units re-joined their garrisons on 3 July, the Soviet and Polish troops were in no rush to leave and remained in Czechoslovakia. On 11 July there were still 16,889 foreign soldiers in Czechoslovakia, along with 4,693 vehicles on the grounds that they were out of order and needed repairs. Although these units did begin to depart, on the morning of 17 July, 14,449 men, 3,858 vehicles, 68 tanks and 43 aircraft and helicopters still remained in Czechoslovakia, and two days later the numbers had only gone down to 11,704 men, 3,041 vehicles, 68 tanks and 23 aircraft and helicopters. It was only on 3 August that the last units of the Soviet 38th Army finally left Czechoslovakia.[48]

Soviet hesitations

At the beginning of July, after the show of force of Exercise Šumava, Moscow still hoped that multilateral negotiations could resolve the Czechoslovak crisis. The CPSU Politburo had adopted a resolution inviting the Czechs to a meeting of the Warsaw Pact countries in the Polish capital on 10 and 11 July "to discuss the situation in Czechoslovakia". The letter of invitation stated that the WTO states did not want to interfere in Czechoslovak internal affairs, but could not accept the country, where the borders of the socialist world crossed, being attacked by "imperialism" which wanted to "destroy the socialist system and change the balance of power in Europe to its advantage".[49] The letter denounced the progress of the counter-revolution which it said was supported by KSČ members, including the Central Committee.[50] On 9 July, the KSČ replied that it preferred to enter into bilateral negotiations rather than go to a general meeting. Finally, during a telephone conversation between Brezhnev and Dubček, the Czechoslovaks refused to go to Warsaw. Prague considered the 'Letter of the Five' an unacceptable interference in the country's internal affairs.[51]

At the Warsaw meeting, in the absence of the Czechoslovak delegation, Gomułka stated that there was no doubt that the process of transforming the socialist state into a capitalist one was under way in Czechoslovakia. As a result, Brezhnev proposed to send a collective letter to the KSČ to organise a bilateral or trilateral meeting to explain the views of the 'Warsaw Five'. He stressed that if the Czechoslovak leaders did not listen to their advice, it would be necessary to continue working to identify 'healthy' forces in the KSČ and look for an opportunity to enable the Party to take the initiative in fighting for the restoration of the KSČ's leading role and the normalisation of the situation in the country. A letter was finally sent to Prague, asking that they "take drastic measures of urgency to avert the onslaught of the enemy, since the defence of socialism in Czechoslovakia is not an internal matter of this country but the sacred duty of the whole socialist community".[52]

Czechoslovak opponents to Dubček's reform policy were now becoming more worried, especially as the September KSČ Congress delegates' elections showed a reformist victory. Time was running out, and they knew that without Soviet backing their cause was lost. It was therefore with the support of the Soviet political leaders, probably through the ambassador Chervonenko, that they organised on 19 June – when there were in Czechoslovakia thousands of WTO soldiers for the Šumava exercise – a meeting of 10,000 members of the People's Militia in a Ruzyně airport hangar. The initial purpose of the meeting was to organise public marches in the cities, where the militiamen would proclaim their determination to fight against "the anti-socialist elements and the threat of counter-revolution" after Prchlík recommended bringing non-communists into the militia, while Husak even proposed its dissolution. However, Dubček and other reformers frustrated the operation by rallying the militiamen to their cause.[53]

On 2 July, Chervonenko was summoned before the CPSU Politburo. In his speech, the ambassador repeated that Dubček and Černík do not intend to fight against the opponents of socialism, adding that there were in the country leaders favourable to the USSR who could replace them. He did not consider it expedient to use force, and he

A column of T-55s of the Hungarian Army during Exercise Šumava in June 1968. Note the MT-55 bridge layer near the rear of the column.

insisted on the need to withdraw the remaining troops stationed in Czechoslovakia following Šumava, because they crystallised popular anger against them.[54] Podgorny, Petro Shelest and Andropov insisted that Soviet forces stayed in Czechoslovakia, but Podgorny, like Kosygin, nevertheless wished that the measures taken correspond to a certain extent to the norms of international law.[55] Andrei Gromyko, the Foreign Minister, was more aggressive and called for effective and rapid action in the form of an armed intervention. Brezhnev, to whom the final decision came back, was cautious and did not want to make any mistake in assessing the situation.[56] The Soviet leader, while still in favour of a political solution to the crisis, nevertheless had to consider the opinions of Politburo members who were increasingly in favour of a military solution.

The next day, the Politburo resumed its meeting. Brezhnev announced that Kádár had informed him that he was now in favour of military intervention. He contacted Gomułka to ask him to write to the Czechoslovak leaders and convene a meeting of the 'Five' in Warsaw for 14 July.[57] By this manoeuvre, he again delayed the military solution of the Czechoslovak problem.

Pressure and threats increased against Prague. After the end of Exercise Šumava, the Soviet government sent a note to their Czechoslovak counterparts on 20 July, accusing them of undermining the solidity of the Warsaw Pact and of not securing their borders with the FRG and Austria.[58] As evidence of insufficient border security, the Soviets used the discovery of a hidden weapons depot in the Sokolov district. This, like many others such examples, was the work of KGB agents infiltrated in Czechoslovakia under the cover of being tourists.[59]

The Soviet media reiterated these accusations in a press campaign against Czechoslovakia. Articles agitated against the threat of the counter-revolution, pushing the need to protect the interests of the socialist countries and to help a fraternal party and its people in defending the achievements of socialism against the dangers posed by the activities of the "imperialist West". The Soviet disinformation campaign also asserted that NATO troops were concentrating on the border with Czechoslovakia, although, apart from conventional exercises, the Czechoslovak intelligence services had not confirmed any increased military activity on the other side of the Iron Curtain. The Soviet press denounced a movement of armoured vehicles of the US Army in Czechoslovakia, with eight M24 Chaffee light tanks, three M3 half-tracked armoured vehicles and three M8 Greyhound armoured vehicles, supplemented by other military equipment from the Second World War. This convoy was not an invention of Soviet propaganda but had arrived in Czechoslovakia on 25 and 26 April from Austria only to participate in the filming of the movie *The Bridge at Remagen*.[60]

While Brezhnev was always anxious to find a political solution to the crisis, the tone of Soviet propaganda now emphasised the Western subversion of Czechoslovakia, an argument already used concerning Hungary in 1956. The media thus prepared public opinion by providing justifications for possible military intervention. Such an operation was also the subject of intense preparations under the camouflage of military exercises.

On 10 July 1968, the Deputy Chief of the WTO Armed Forces met the GDR Defence Minister, General Heinz Hoffmann, and agreed with him on the organisation of a joint exercise on the Czechoslovakian border, with the agreement of GDR leader Ulbricht. On the same day, General Ivan Tutarinov, Permanent Representative of the WTO Armed Forces in the Hungarian Army, made the same request to Colonel Lajos Czineg. During this exercise, the Hungarian Army was to employ the 8th Motorised Rifle Division, located at Zalaegerszeg along the border with Yugoslavia, under the command of General Bela Lakatos in the north of Hungary.[61] It was one of the best divisions in the Hungarian Army, equipped with modern T-54 and T-55 tanks.

Final Preparations

These multiple exercises were in fact only lures for Operation Danube, which was by then considered imminent, as shown by a meeting organised by Defence Minister Grechko with the Soviet commanders and the CoS in Moscow, where the plan of the operation was defined and approved.[62] He discussed the details of the invasion with the

Wojciech Jaruzekski, emerged as Minister of Defence of Poland after removing and persecuting several contesters in 1968. While subsequently leading several purges at home, and then emerging as the de-facto military dictator of Poland in 1981, decades later, he was to describe the military intervention in Czechoslovakia as a 'political and moral mistake'.

A Polish-operated OT-64 armoured personnel carrier crossing a river via a pontoon bridge during Exercise Šumava.

OPERATION DANUBE: SOVIET AND WARSAW PACT INTERVENTION IN CZECHOSLOVAKIA, 1968

One of the first combat vehicles of the Soviet Army to go into action during Operation Danube was the ASU-57: a small and light assault gun designed for use by the VDV, which entered service in 1959. Powered by a 50hp civilian car engine located at the front, it was protected by only 6mm of aluminium armour, had a completely open top, and weighted about 4,000kg. Its primary 'protection' was its high mobility: the ASU-57 could barely protect its crew from rifle-calibre bullets, but could reach a speed of 45km/h. Armament consisted of a 57mm Ch-51 (later Ch-51M) L/73 gun and one 7.62mm anti-aircraft machine gun. 54 ASU-57s were assigned to each VDV division, with an anti-tank company of nine in each parachute regiment. Vehicles deployed by the 103rd Guards Airborne Division during Operation Danube were all painted in dark olive green overall and wore the large VDV-insignia and turret numbers in white on their sides. (Artwork by David Bocquelet)

The ASU-85 was an assault gun designed to replace the ASU-57. Based on the chassis of the PT-76 amphibious tank, it mounted a 85mm D-70 gun – with limited anti-tank capability – and a coaxially mounted 7.62mm machine gun. Each VDV division had one battalion of 18 such vehicles, which was usually held centrally and detached as required by the situation. All the ASU-85s deployed during Operation Danube were painted in dark olive green overall. However, all received the white identification stripe down their superstructure – in addition to their usual turret numbers. (Artwork by David Bocquelet)

One of the first vehicles to be seen on the streets of Prague were the PT-76 amphibious light tanks. Its designation was derived from the calibre of its main armament: the 76.2mm D-56T series rifled gun. The PT-76 – the hull of which was quite bulky to achieve buoyancy – was used as the standard reconnaissance tank of the WTO's armies and although not part of the order of battle of the 7th and 103rd Guards Airborne Divisions was frequently seen in close support of the VDV troops on the streets of Prague during the intervention of 21 August 1968. As usual, all the vehicles were painted in dark olive green overall and wore white identification stripes down the front hull and turret sides. (Artwork by David Bocquelet)

The BRDM-1 was the standard amphibious armoured scout car of most of the WTO's mechanised formations in the 1960s. At least 10,000 were manufactured from 1957 to 1966, and they served in company-sized detachment assigned to the reconnaissance battalion of every division, with the task of reconnaissance and screening. Visible at the bottom of the chassis, between main wheels, are additional chain-driven belly wheels, lowered by the driver to allow trench crossing. Standard armament included one 7.62mm medium machine gun, but up to three of these could be installed. As usual for the 1960s, all were painted in dark olive green overall: vehicles deployed during Operation Danube all wore white vertical identification stripes in addition to their turret numbers. (Artwork by David Bocquelet)

Based on the chassis of the PT-76 amphibious tank, the BTR-50 was an APC with a crew of two, and was primarily assigned to the Motorised Rifle troops of the tank formations of the Soviet Army in the 1960s. Standard armament included one 7.62mm machine gun, but there were many variants and some had as many as three machine guns. A variation of the type was manufactured in Czechoslovakia as the OT-62. Like all other combat vehicles of the WTO during Operation Danube, all were painted in dark olive green overall, and wore vertical identification stripes in white, along with other tactical insignia. (Artwork by David Bocquelet)

The standard main battle tank of the Soviet, Polish, Hungarian, Bulgarian and East German armies of the 1960s was the T-54/55 family, of which there were at least seven major production variants, some of which were manufactured in Poland and Czechoslovakia. By 1968, many were upgraded through the addition of infra-red searchlights to the right of their 100mm D-10T main gun. This example was operated by one of the Soviet Army's tank formations deployed to secure downtown Prague on 21 August 1968. While painted in dark olive green overall, it received white identification stripes down the front hull and turret sides, in addition to an entire set of turret markings. (Artwork by David Bocquelet)

OPERATION DANUBE: SOVIET AND WARSAW PACT INTERVENTION IN CZECHOSLOVAKIA, 1968

Still relatively new into service as of 1968 was the T-62 main battle tank. Based on a stretched chassis and the same powerplant as the T-54/55 family but armed with a new 115mm U-5TS smoothbore gun, it eventually saw widespread use in tank formations. Deployed only by Soviet Army units during Operation Danube, in the longer term it did not prove to be an outstanding success and was subsequently replaced by the T-64/T-72/T-80 series. This example belonged to a tank unit deployed in the Prague area: it was painted in dark olive green overall, and – in addition to the usual turret number – wore vertical identification stripes in white. (Artwork by David Bocquelet)

Developed towards the end of the Second World War, but too late to see action in that conflict, the IS-3 heavy tank (IS stood for Iosif Stalin, the Russian form of Joseph Stalin) had well-sloped armour and a semi-hemispherical cast turret, which became the hallmark of all subsequent Soviet tanks. The version deployed during Operation Danube was the slightly modernised IS-3M, which included additional jettisonable external fuel tanks, improved hull welding, and a 12.7mm DShK heavy machine gun for anti-aircraft defence. All were painted in dark olive green (or dark green) overall and received a set of vertical white identification stripes in addition to their turret numbers. (Artwork by David Bocquelet)

The T-10M heavy tank was the final development of the IS tank series. In comparison to its predecessor, it received a longer hull with additional road wheels, a larger turret mounting and a new 122mm M-62-T2 gun with a five-baffle muzzle brake. Originally designated IS-10, it was accepted to service in 1953 under the designation T-10 as part of the de-Stalinisation process: through the mid-1960s large numbers remained in service with units of the 2nd strategic echelon, deployed in western USSR. All T-10Ms deployed during Operation Danube were painted in dark olive overall, and most received the white identification stripe down the turret and the hull. (Artwork by David Bocquelet)

Perhaps the rarest armoured combat vehicle deployed by the Soviet Army during Operation Danube was the SU-122-54 – a self-propelled tank destroyer equipped with the 122mm M-62T gun installed on the T-54-chassis, intended to provide long-range fire-support. Only 100 of these were manufactured, in two sub-variants, in the 1955-57 period: both had a crew of five, and carried 35 rounds of 122mm high-explosive-fragmenting and anti-tank ammunition. It seems that only one battalion of 20 such vehicles was deployed during Operation Danube: all were left in dark olive green overall, and received the white identification stripe down their sides, in addition to the usual turret numbers. (Artwork by David Bocquelet)

The D-442 FUG amphibious reconnaissance vehicle was the Hungarian-designed and manufactured equivalent to the Soviet BRDM-1 armoured scout car, development of which was prompted by the Soviet failure to fulfil the promise of supplying large numbers of old BA-65s at low price. Lightly armoured (13mm at the front and 7mm at sides and rear), it was mainly intended for reconnaissance duties. If installed, armament consisted of either 7.62mm UK light machine gun or 14.5mm KPVT heavy machine guns. In addition to the Hungarian Army, small numbers were exported to Bulgaria, Czechoslovakia, East Germany and Poland, which also used them for forward artillery observation tasks. Hungarian D-442s deployed during Operation Danube were painted in dark olive green overall, and wore white dots as means of identification, in addition to their white turret numbers. (Artwork by David Bocquelet)

The 8th Motorised Rifle Division – nominally the best unit of the Hungarian Army, home-based at Zalaegerszeg, near the border with Yugoslavia – was deployed in Czechoslovakia during Exercise Šumava: it returned to the country only two months later, while participating in Operation Danube. All the armoured battalions of the 8th Motorised Rifle Division were equipped with T-55 main battle tanks that, as of 1968, lacked the turret-mounted 12.7mm DShK heavy machine guns. All were painted in dark olive green overall and wore the usual set of markings typical for Hungarian formations: a white dot, followed by a three-digit tactical number. (Artwork by David Bocquelet)

OPERATION DANUBE: SOVIET AND WARSAW PACT INTERVENTION IN CZECHOSLOVAKIA, 1968

The standard armoured personnel carrier of the motorised rifle divisions of the Polish Army of the late 1960s was the Czechoslovak-designed and manufactured OT-64 SKOT. Originally intended to replace the OT-810 halftrack, based on the German Sd.Kfz.251, this entered service in Czechoslovakia in 1963, and was manufactured under licence in Poland. Roughly comparable to the Soviet-made BTR-60 eight-wheeled APC, it used a diesel instead of petrol engine, and had an armoured hull, with an entrance via twin doors at the rear. Primary armament of the illustrated variant consisted of a 14.5mm KPV machine gun, with a 7.62mm PKT machine gun installed coaxially, both in a one-man turret similar to the one installed on the BTR-60PB and the subsequent BRDM-2. Polish OT-64s frequently wore the national insignia on their forward hulls: sometimes, this was applied in full colour, as shown here, but other times only in the form of an outline. (Artwork by David Bocquelet)

As with the Soviet, Hungarian, Bulgarian, East German and Czechoslovak mechanised formations, the standard main battle tank of Polish tank units was the T-54/55 family: indeed, as in Czechoslovakia, this was locally manufactured from 1956. Painted in dark olive green overall, Polish-operated examples were easy to recognise not only by their national insignia, usually applied on the forward sides of their turrets, but especially by their large, four-digit tactical numbers. During Operation Danube, they received vertical identification stripes in white, applied down their hull front and turret sides. (Artwork by David Bocquelet)

The standard medium, self-propelled anti-aircraft artillery piece of the Soviet and East German armies of the late 1960s was the ZSU-57-2: essentially a lighter variant of the T-54-chassis, mounting twin 57mm S-60 autocannons – the most powerful anti-aircraft gun installed on a self-propelled chassis at the time – in an open-topped, box-like welded turret. Contrary to the T-54, the vehicle was lightly armoured (13.5-15mm on hull front and sides, and 13.5mm on the turret). Two batteries of four ZSU-57-2s were assigned to every tank regiment, but relatively few saw service in motorised rifle formations. As usual, all were painted in dark olive green and received vertical identification stripes in white for the duration of Operation Danube. (Artwork by David Bocquelet)

v

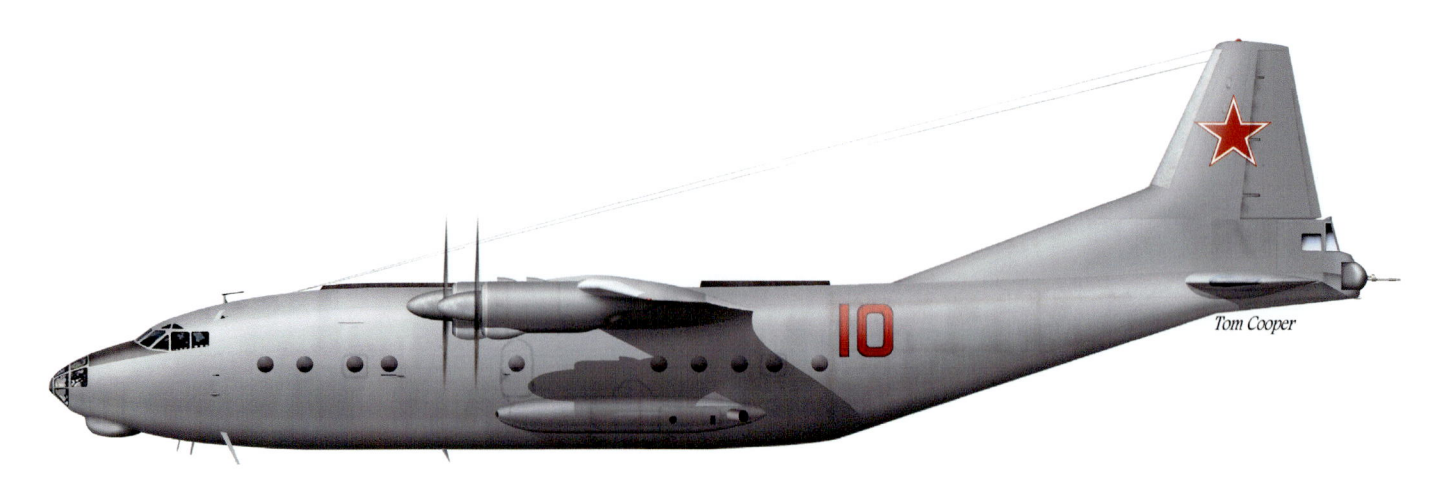

The most widely used transport aircraft of Operation Danube was the Antonov An-12, about 440 of which were deployed in support of the 7th and 103rd Guards Airborne Divisions of the Soviet Army. Except for a few examples drawn from the Soviet national airline, Aeroflot, all of the aircraft operated by the Soviet Transport Aviation were painted in mid-grey overall and wore very few markings. National markings – in the form of red stars – were applied in six positions (though sometimes replaced by the flag of the USSR on the fin), and famous two-digit 'bort' numbers in red – usually outlined in white, but sometimes in dark blue or black – on the rear fuselage. (Artwork by Tom Cooper)

Giant Mil Mi-6 helicopters of the 688th Independent Helicopter Regiment, V-VS (home-based at Legnica AB in Poland) were deployed in support of the 7th Guards Airborne Division of the Soviet Army during Operation Danube. They usually carried equipment, ammunition, and food and even brought in several BTR-152 armoured personnel carriers. As far as is known, all were painted in medium grey overall, and wore relatively few other markings: the latter included their big red bort numbers (outlined in white), and national markings in the form of big red stars applied on the rear fuselage. Contrary to the much smaller Mi-4s, they are not known to have received red identification stripes around their booms. (Artwork by Luca Canossa)

Soviet tactical combat aircraft of the 1960s wore no camouflage patterns. Instead, all were painted in the factory in two layers of clear lacquer, mixed with 5% and 10% aluminium powder, respectively. This resulted in the colour colloquially known as 'silver grey'. MiG-17F and Su-7B fighter-bombers, MiG-21 interceptors and Yak-28s deployed during Operation Danube also received two red identification stripes around their booms. The example shown here was a MiG-21PF deployed to one of the air bases in Czechoslovakia from August until November 1968. It is illustrated as armed with R-3S (ASCC/NATO-codenamed 'AA-2 Atoll') infra-red homing air-to-air missiles. (Artwork by Tom Cooper)

OPERATION DANUBE: SOVIET AND WARSAW PACT INTERVENTION IN CZECHOSLOVAKIA, 1968

A member of a Soviet T-55 crew, shown wearing the typical 'tank costume' (*tankoviy kostyum*, colloquially 'TK'). Essentially an overall made of fire-resistant material, the TK was intended for all Soviet vehicle operators and was in widespread use during the Cold War, as combat and working dress. Other characteristic items of his uniform include *kirzach* (high boots) and the standard tankers' 'summer' helmet, similar to the one worn during the Second World War, but with different earmuffs and a quick-attachment jack for intercom. His weapon is an AKS-47 assault rifle, with downward-folding metal stock, custom-tailored for use in the cramped insides of armoured vehicles, but also issued to paratroopers. (Artwork by Anderson Subtil)

This private of the 12th Motorised Rifle Regiment of the Bulgarian People's Army is shown in the standard Bulgarian Army Brown wool uniform JKT29, strongly reminiscent of the First World War, but still worn to the late 1980s. His equipment was limited to a blanket roll, a leather belt for his German-made flask left-over from the Second World War, and a large pouch for the magazines of his AK-47 assault rifle. Notable is the traditional Bulgarian field cap with the red star and national colours, with integral ear and neck flaps. (Artwork by Anderson Subtil)

This light machine gunner of the 7th Guards Airborne Division is shown wearing the summer cotton twill jumpsuit created especially for the Soviet airborne troops (*Vozdushno-Desantye Voyska*, VDV). The soldiers of 7th Guards Airborne Division wore the newly introduced cornflower blue beret that would later become iconic of the VDV. This initially caused confusion amongst some local civilians who mistook the VDV troopers for UN peacekeepers. The 317th Guards Airborne Regiment of the 103rd Guards Airborne Division entered Czechoslovakia wearing the short-lived burgundy coloured beret. Another typical issue was his *telnyashka* (t-shirt in navy blue and white stripes). During Operation Danube, VDV-troops carried only basic equipment, like the 6x3 bayonet (with its wire-cutter sheath) and a pouch for the drum magazines of his RPK – which was a light machine gun version of the AKM assault rifle. (Artwork by Anderson Subtil)

This young recruit of the ČSLA is shown wearing the initial version of the 'rain drop pattern' field uniform, including a field cap with integral ear and neck flaps, which replaced the multi-colour 'clown' pattern in the late 1950s. Usually, Czechoslovak troops wore grey shirts underneath, and traditional jackboots, although more modern (and more comfortable) shoes were available. His equipment includes a black leather belt and a pouch for magazines for the vz. 58 assault rifle: while similar to the AK family, the latter was a different design based on an original operating system. (Artwork by Anderson Subtil)

vii

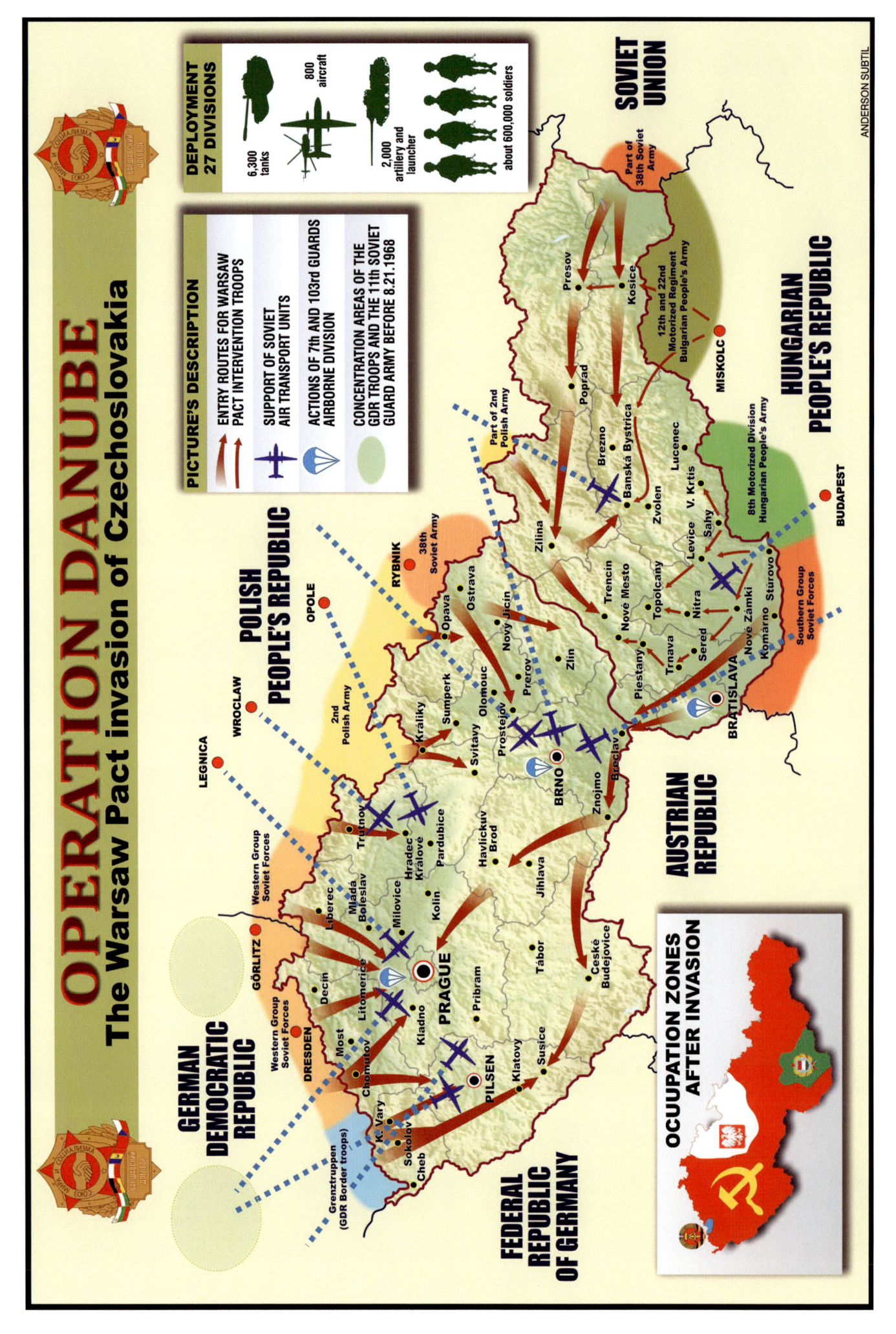

OPERATION DANUBE
The Warsaw Pact invasion of Czechoslovakia

Troops of the 11th Motorised Rifle Division with their vehicles near the border with Czechoslovakia before the start of the invasion: not only their trucks, but even their helmets were soon to receive vertical white strips used for easier identification of friendly forces. Ultimately, they were not to take part in the occupation, but remained near the border in a state of readiness.

leaders of the Southern Group of Forces in Moscow, particularly the occupation of Bratislava and Brno. A Hungarian division was to be ready east of the Danube on 25 July, while the 93rd and 254th Motorised Rifle Divisions and the Soviet 13th Tank Division were to cross the three bridges at Bratislava, Medveďov and Komárno and head towards Bratislava–Brno. NVA representatives met Marshal Yakubovsky on 25 July in Legnica, Poland. The East German units were supposed to mainly provide logistical facilities for Soviet troops operating from the GDR. The NVA 7th Armoured Division, under the command of Major General Werner Winter, then passed under the command of the Soviet 20th Army, while the NVA 11th Motorised Rifle Division of Colonel Erich Dirwelis remained in GSFG reserve.[63]

On 14 July, when Polish troops finally withdrew from Czechoslovakia after Exercise Šumava, the commander of the Silesian Military District, General Florian Siwicki, was ordered by Defence Minister Jaruzelski to prepare his troops for an exercise to be held in southern Poland. He mobilised for this the 4th Motorised Rifle Division and the 10th and 11th Tank Divisions. These divisions were to be supported by the 58th Fighter Aviation Regiment. On 25 July, Jaruzelski received from Yakubovsky a detailed description of the missions for the Polish Army. The aim, he was told, was to provide assistance to the KSČ to break the counter-revolutionary danger. Regarding the Czech Army, Yakubovsky said that "if the ČSLA troops accept the entrance of friendly troops with understanding, it is necessary to establish cooperation with them and carry out the tasks that are assigned. If smaller individual units move to the counter-revolution side, they must be located and then disarmed. Open fire if fired upon by an opponent."[64]

On the basis of Yakubovsky's instructions, on 27 July, Jaruzelski ordered the military exercise to be completed. On 28 July and the morning of 29 July, three Polish divisions took up their starting positions. Soviet trains also crossed into Poland on 28 July, carrying the 1st and 18th Guards Motorised Rifle Divisions and the 11th Guards Army. A total of about 2,658 wagons and more than 600 vehicles arrived in Poland until 20 August, as well as an undetermined number of Soviet helicopters that used the Wroclaw and Mierzecice air bases.[65]

The proliferation of military exercises made possible the setting up of the necessary infrastructure for Operation Danube. For example, during Exercise Nemen, which took place from 24 July to 10 August in the western regions of the USSR, Soviet forces transported thousands of tons of ammunition and fuel to the border. They also mobilised thousands of reservists and concentrated troops all along the border. As part of this exercise, on 23 July, the Bulgarian 12th Motorised Rifle Regiment crossed the Soviet frontier to come under the command of the 128th Soviet Motorised Rifle Division, while on 27 July, the Bulgarian 22nd Motorised Rifle Regiment arrived in the

Czechoslovak-made OT-64 armoured personnel carriers were the primary troop transports of the 4th Motorised Rifle Division of the Polish Army. This photograph shows a pair of vehicles camouflaged with foliage in July 1968.

USSR by air, equipped with heavy weapons and BTR-60PB armoured personnel carriers.

At the end of July, Soviet officers of the Airborne and Military Transport Aviation, wearing Aeroflot civilian uniforms, arrived in Prague and Brno to conduct reconnaissance of airports and landing strips that could receive Antonov AN-12 transport aircraft. These visits allowed them to select the airports of Ruzyně and Tuřany for a possible disembarkation of troops. Meanwhile, the Soviet 7th and 103rd Guards Airborne Divisions, comprising about 13,000 men, received orders on the night of 29/30 July to return to their bases ready for operations.[66]

Brezhnev's Last-Ditch Attempt

In late July, the invasion seemed close but Brezhnev still wanted to resolve the crisis through negotiations. On 19 July, during the CPSU Politburo meeting, he said that time was not in Moscow's favour. He feared a rapprochement between Dubček, Yugoslavia's Tito and Ceaucescu in Romania, while the French and Italian Communist Parties, who were in favour of the KSČ, called for a meeting of the European Communist Parties where there was a great risk of seeing Prague's position approved. However, Brezhnev asked that all possible political solutions be exhausted before taking military measures to settle the Czechoslovak problem. Kosygin supported him and believed that a form of effective political pressure could be a bilateral meeting. Such a position had not, however, met with majority support within the Politburo against supporters of more radical measures. In the final analysis, the Soviet leadership agreed with Brezhnez and decided to hold a last-chance meeting with the Czechoslovak leaders.

Nevertheless, in accordance with the Politburo decisions of 19 and 22 July, the political preparations for the invasion continued: between 20 and 26 July, the Soviet leadership wrote a 'Declaration of the Political Bureau of the KSČ Central Committee and the Revolutionary Government of the Czechoslovak Socialist Republic on Domestic and Foreign Policy' and the 'Appeal to the citizens of Czechoslovakia and the Czechoslovak army'. These documents were to be made public after the entry into Czechoslovakia of the WTO troops in an attempt to justify the invasion.[67] Grechko and Yakubovsky returned hastily from a visit to Algiers. They completed the latest details of the plan for Operation Danube, which were approved at a meeting convened in Moscow on 23 July. The order was given for the military units to be ready to carry out the assigned tasks by the morning of 29 July, at the moment when the last negotiations between the Czechoslovak and Soviet leaders were to take place.[68]

The Čierna nad Tisou and Bratislava meetings

The final talks took place at Čierna nad Tisou, near the border of the Soviet Union and Czechoslovakia, in the middle of tobacco fields. This unusual location was chosen to indicate the dramatic nature of the meeting and to exert psychological pressure on the Prague leaders. It had previously been prepared by the KGB so that Czechoslovak officials were cut off from the rest of the country, even though the negotiations were taking place on their own territory. While the KSČ leaders did not have the opportunity to get in touch with the Party apparatus in Prague, the Soviet delegation had a team of specialists who focused solely on reading the Czechoslovak press, thus giving the Soviet representatives the latest information, which they then skilfully used at the meeting.[69] The Soviet leaders emerged as a perfectly co-ordinated team, while the Czechoslovak delegation, despite its efforts, did not seem so united. The Czechs nevertheless benefited from one asset, the support of the population, after an appeal by Czech novelist and Prague Spring supporter Pavel Kohout was published in the press on 26 July, becoming the basis of a petition signed by more than a million people.[70]

In Čierna nad Tisou, the Soviets put pressure on the Czechoslovaks to make concessions and change their position. Dubček began by denying the accusations made in the letter of the 'Warsaw Five'. He not only refused to change his political agenda but denounced external pressures that he said did not conform to the standards of relations between allies. He warned the Soviets that only "knowing that you respect our sovereignty allows our joint action against imperialism".[71] In reply, in a four-hour speech, Brezhnev reiterated all his criticism of the Czechoslovak leaders and the reform process, saying that there was a counter-revolutionary situation in their country. Above all, he warned, Dubček's policy threatened the security of the WTO countries, so it was no longer a purely Czechoslovak affair. He also claimed that the western border of Czechoslovakia was open, and that weapons had been smuggled through it. This then created a situation, he said, that was threatening to the Czechoslovak leaders, who might be swept away by superior forces. Other Soviet representatives at the meeting were more brutal and insulting, forcing Kosygin to apologise on behalf of his delegation.[72]

The meeting ended, however, with a new speech by Brezhnev, which was reassuring in tone, and to everyone's surprise the tension between Prague and Moscow seemed to have fallen away. Brezhnev even stated that:

> …a broad and fraternal exchange of views took place on issues of mutual interest to the two parties […] The negotiations of the CPSU Politburo and the KSČ Central Committee took place in an atmosphere of expression of openness, honesty and mutual understanding on how to develop and consolidate the traditional friendly relations between the communist parties and the peoples of our countries, on the basis of the principles of Marxism-Leninism and proletarian internationalism.[73]

Despite this consensual discourse, no written document was signed at the end of the meetings. There were doubts whether Dubček and Brezhnev reached any agreement that the Czechoslovak leaders promised to regain control of the media, to dissolve the political clubs and organisations formed since January and to sack the most radical reformers.[74] According to Dubček, even if the Soviets put forward these requirements, the Czechoslovakians did not promise anything. They committed themselves only to fighting the excesses of the press and reaffirmed their attachment to socialism and their loyalty to their country's obligations under the Warsaw Pact. They also agreed to reaffirm their position at a further meeting in Bratislava in the presence of the other WTO member countries.

The last hope for a peaceful settlement of the crisis therefore took place in the Slovak capital. At this conference, Brezhnev read to Dubček a draft joint statement, prepared by the Soviets.[75] It appeared conciliatory, since it contained no assertion about the risk of a counter-revolution in Czechoslovakia. In very general terms, it also recalled the respect of the general laws of socialist construction, the leading role of the Party, the principle of democratic centralism, the struggle against bourgeois ideology, the close links existing within the WTO and the fraternal mutual help and solidarity between the socialist countries. But the main point of the 'Bratislava Declaration' was the provision on the protection of the achievements of socialism as an international duty of all socialist countries. However, it was a rather vague thesis, allowing different interpretations. In particular, it made it possible to consider using, if necessary, coercive measures – including military ones – to defend these gains.

Upon leaving the Bratislava meeting, each side considered itself satisfied. Dubček believed he now had the right to pursue the Czechoslovak path towards socialism; but he was wrong. Recognising the defence of socialism concerned the entire socialist community, the declaration gave the right to sister parties to discuss, and if necessary to intervene in by force, the internal affairs of his country.

5
THE ROAD TO INVASION

At the beginning of August 1968, it seemed the climax of the conflict between Czechoslovakia and the 'Warsaw Five' had passed. But the Bratislava conference was based on a misunderstanding. For Dubček, it authorised the continuation of the reforms, notwithstanding some corrections as to its scale and pace, whereas for Brezhnev, it signalled a recovery in the country by the KSČ, including the restriction of press freedom and the prohibition of non-communist political groups. Brezhnev was once again betting that Dubček would finally align himself with the Kremlin's position. When he realised his mistake, his only remaining option was to start Operation Danube.

The international context of the Czechoslovak crisis

The Soviet decision to intervene militarily in Czechoslovakia was part of a particular strategic and international context. Soviet policy towards Czechoslovakia was largely dominated by the USSR's strategic situation in the late 1960s. When Brezhnev seized power in Moscow, his country's international position was weakened following the crises in Berlin in 1961 and Cuba in 1962. Above all, he inherited the break between USSR, Albania and the People's Republic of China. The tension with Beijing continued to grow throughout the 1960s, leading to clashes on the Usuri River and in Central Asia in 1969. Moscow was therefore militarily reinforcing its eastern borders throughout the decade, but now needed to secure its position on its western borders and prohibit NATO from taking advantage of the difficulties it faced in the Far East to launch a possible attack in Europe. In this situation, the Kremlin wanted to leave no doubt about its domination of Eastern Europe at the moment when it deployed its *détente* policy during the East–West talks. From the Soviet point of view, it was consequently absolutely vital to point out that any improvement in relations with the West could not be interpreted by any of its satellites as a weakening of its influence in Central Europe.

Some of the Czechoslovak international moves in 1968 suggested that Prague was emerging from Moscow's orbit with a rapprochement with Bonn, which materialised in the signing of two trade agreements with West Germany. Although Czechoslovakia was the last country in the Eastern Bloc, except the GDR, to sign such agreements with the FRG, in the context of the Prague Spring it might seem like a first step in breaking ties with the socialist states.[1] The rapprochement of Czechoslovakia with Romania and Yugoslavia was another important moment in Prague's international policy. From 9–11 August, a delegation led by Josip Broz Tito, followed by a Ceausescu-led Romanian delegation from 15–17 August, visited the Czech capital. Since 1948, Yugoslavia had been outside the direct influence of the Soviet Union, while Romania had succeeded in reducing its involvement in the WTO and its foreign policy was also more independent. The USSR could, therefore, fear the creation of a neutral socialist bloc uniting Prague, Bucharest and Belgrade, a prospect that would not please Hungary and Kádár, who might find themselves isolated.[2] The loss of Czechoslovakia was thus perceived by the Kremlin as an existential threat. Whereas the democratic principles upheld by Dubček, and even his conception of socialism with a human face, could be tolerated, the loss of control of the country could not.

US Position

A military intervention in Czechoslovakia, however, ran the risk of a deterioration of the USSR's situation on the international scene. Moscow feared the reaction of the West and a challenge to the *détente* policy. The concentration of a large number of troops in Poland and the GDR to invade Czechoslovakia could also suggest to NATO that the Warsaw Pact was preparing to launch an attack in the West at the risk of triggering a new world war. It was therefore crucial for Moscow to choose the right moment to inform the West – and first and foremost the United States – of their intention.

Dubček meeting Yugoslav leader Josip Broz Tito on 9 August 1968. Good relations between Prague and Belgrade, and then between Prague and Bucharest, created fears in Moscow about a possible loss of control over Czechoslovakia.

Not interested: preoccupied with civil rights-related issues at home, the Vietnam War and negotiations for the Non-Proliferation Treaty and SALT abroad, the US leaders showed no interest in developments in Czechoslovakia in 1967-1968. President Lyndon B Johnson (right) with Secretary of State Dean Rusk, are seen speaking during a cabinet meeting on 9 February 1968. (Lyndon B Johnson Presidential Library)

In 1968, Washington did not care about Czechoslovakia. The US was too busy with the Vietnam War and the protests against its involvement in the conflict, the racial problem and the upcoming presidential elections, to say nothing of the murders of Martin Luther King Jr on 4 April and Senator Robert Kennedy on 6 June. For President Lyndon B. Johnson's administration, the priorities of international policy were the Vietnam War, talks on the reduction of nuclear weapons, the reorganisation of NATO after the withdrawal of France from its military structures and the improvement of its relations with the People's Republic of China. Above all, it was keen to continue bilateral talks with Moscow, particularly to push North Vietnam to start peace negotiations. *Détente* was also reflected in the decrease of Western troops in the FRG. American manpower in Europe was reduced from more than 400,000 in 1962 to less than 300,000 in 1968, while more than half a million Americans were in Vietnam in 1968. Other NATO member states had also reduced their units in West Germany, as Belgium withdrew two of its six brigades and Britain cut the number of its soldiers from 53,000 to 48,000.[3]

The United States remained relatively silent on events in Czechoslovakia. The only exceptions were Under Secretary for Political Affairs Eugen Rostow's statement of 28 April and Spokesperson for the US Department of State Robert McCloskey's statement of 2 May on 'US sympathy for developments in Czechoslovakia'. Consequently, Soviet leaders had no clear idea of the attitude that the US and NATO would take in the event of military intervention and how this would affect US–Soviet relations.[4] In this context, Johnson's attitude became clearer in the summer of 1968. His main concern was to start the SALT (Strategic Arms Limitation Talks) negotiations as soon as possible and to meet with Soviet Prime Minister Kosygin before the US presidential elections in November. The United States was therefore very cautious at the height of the Czechoslovak crisis. Secretary of State Dean Rusk responded to the Bavarian Franz Josef Strauss, the GDR's Minister of Finance, who asked him how the US would behave in case of invasion, with a simple "nothing". Henry Kissinger – a future US Secretary of State – said much the same thing to Czechoslovak Foreign Minister Jiří Hájek during a visit to Prague. Rusk declared on 22 July that his government did not want to be involved in one way or another in Czechoslovak events. Rostow said: "We are working hard to avoid giving the impression of encouraging what is happening in Czechoslovakia, [or] the matters of its Party and its government." In Moscow, Soviet leaders thus understood that the implementation of a military operation against Prague would not lead to active opposition by the United States. Washington's position could be explained by the Americans' fear that interference in events in Czechoslovakia could be seen as a violation of the division of Europe endorsed at the Yalta Conference in 1945, which would weaken the chances of reaching an agreement on the limitation of strategic nuclear weapons.[5] The Kremlin finally received confirmation of the US position on Czechoslovakia when, in a letter of 18 August, President Johnson told Brezhnev that Washington did not wish to interfere in the Czechoslovak question.[6]

Meanwhile, the Prague reformers were counting on help from the West and the USSR's fears about the reaction of world public opinion to an invasion. The Czechoslovak experience was well received by France and especially the FRG, while the KSČ received enthusiastic support from the Western European Communist Parties. Representatives of the French Communist Party, Waldeck Rochet, and the Italian Communist Party, Luigi Longo, told Brezhnev of their total opposition to military intervention. However, the grumbling of the comrades of Western Europe carried little influence in the event of the loss of Czechoslovakia.

The end of Brezhnev's illusions

Reassured of Washington's intentions regarding a military intervention against Prague, the Kremlin was nevertheless pressed for time. It had to intervene before the KSČ Congress scheduled for 9 September. According to the Soviet analysts' forecasts, it was during the congress that the reforming elements of the Czechoslovak leadership would win a decisive victory, at the expense of the last pro-Moscow cadres.

Dubček's opponents in the KSČ were also increasingly worried and, manipulated in part by the KGB and the Soviet ambassador, were demanding Kremlin intervention. At Čierna na Tisou, KSČ official Antonin Kapek had already sent Brezhnev a letter asking for "fraternal help".[7] At the conference in Bratislava, through the First Secretary of the Ukrainian Communist Party Central Committee, Piotr Shelest, and at Bil'ak's request, a letter was addressed to Brezhnev by members of the KSČ Central Committee, Bil'ak, Dragomir Kolder, Oldrich Shvestka, Kapek and Aloiz Indra. In this letter, written in Cyrillic, the KSČ conservatives asked for "real help" to provide Moscow with a pretext for the intervention of the Warsaw Pact.[8] According to them, the media were in the hands of right-wing forces and were contributing to the development of nationalism and chauvinism, as well as the spread of anti-Soviet and anti-communist feelings in the country. At the same time, they admitted that the KSČ leadership

A MiG-21PFM of the 168th Fighter Aviation Regiment, V-VS, as seen on arrival at a Polish air base 'near the border to Czechoslovakia' in August 1968.

had made a number of mistakes, for example in failing to enforce Marxist-Leninist norms and preventing attacks on socialism, the existence of which was threatened in Czechoslovakia. Their final argument to justify the request for help concerned the favourable conditions created by the right-wing forces to organise a counter-revolutionary coup. The power of the state and the political means likely to prevent it were already paralysed, they claimed. At the end of the letter, they added that they would try to fight on their own, but in the event of failure, would rely on the USSR.[9]

Immediately after the Bratislava meeting, Brezhnev went on holiday in Crimea, but the Kremlin passed on information to him about the situation in Czechoslovakia.[10] He also received information directly from his ambassador in Prague, and through this, he was in contact with the Czechoslovakian conservatives. The latter let him know that Dubček's administration interpreted the results of the Bratislava conference in a completely different way from the leaders of the other Communist parties. On 9 August, in a telephone conversation, Brezhnev told Dubček of his fears that Czechoslovaks were not complying with previous agreements. He therefore asked again that measures be taken to muzzle the media and put an end to the activities of the Social Democratic Party and the political clubs.[11]

On 12 August, a meeting was held in Karlovy Vary between Dubček and Ulbricht, which was organised at the request of Brezhnev to verify whether the KSČ respected the agreements concluded in Bratislava and Čierna nad Tisou.[12] Dubček reported on his country's political

Soviet armament specialists unloading a FAB-50M54 bomb from its transport package.

developments, while Ulbricht took on the role of critic. At the end of the meeting, Ulbricht informed Brezhnev that the KSČ management was not prepared to respect the agreements reached over the past weeks and that it had opened secret relations with the FRG, with whom negotiations were in progress.[13]

The session of the KSČ Central Committee began on 13 August. Its purpose was to discuss the preparations for the federal organisation of the country and the arranging of the next KSČ Congress. It was during this meeting that Brezhnev had a further telephone conversation with Dubček, asking him for explanations concerning anti-Soviet attacks in the Czechoslovak press. Dubček evoked the change of circumstances and the inability to solve the problems raised during previous meetings.[14] Moscow thus felt it became pointless to continue negotiating with the Czechoslovak reformers. Brezhnev believed they would quickly be swept away by a more radical liberal wave that would lead to the restoration of the bourgeois order in Czechoslovakia. He no longer had any doubt about the inevitability of a military invasion.

The last military preparations

Meanwhile, preparations for Operation Danube continued. From 12–15 August, negotiations took place in Yalta which led to the agreement of Hungarian officials for the intervention of their troops in Czechoslovakia. Marshal Grechko travelled to Ukraine on 12 August, to the GDR on 13 August and to Poland on 14 August to give the latest instructions to the military. The Soviet Air Force was preparing to play its role in the invasion. In Moscow, the commander of the 14th Air Army, General Jefimov, mobilised his forces, while in Lvov, the 131st Mixed Aviation Division and its Chief of Operations, Lieutenant Colonel Zdobnikov, prepared the movement of the AN-12s to serve the airports of Prague-Ruzyně, Vodochody, Brno-Tuřany and Náměšad nad Oslavou. The 92nd, 159th, 168th and 192nd Fighter Aviation Regiments, equipped with MiG-21PF/PFMs and MiG-19Ss, were sent to Polish air bases near the Czechoslovakian border.[15]

From his discussions in Poland and the GDR, Grechko concluded that the troops could no longer wait and a decision had to be made quickly. The CPSU Central Committee therefore met again on 16 and 17 August in the Kremlin to decide to launch the intervention. Brezhnev was one of the last to oppose the use of force. This situation was confirmed by the Defence Minister, Grechko, who said in December 1968:

Leonid Ilyich [Brezhnev] did not intend to send troops. For many reasons. There are also Hungarian events. They are fresh in the memories. And the risk of triggering a great war […] But it was impossible for us to lose Czechoslovakia! And it was not only the events in Czechoslovakia that pushed him to send troops; Ulbricht, Gomułka and Zhivkov pressed him daily, and finally Kádár asked him to introduce troops into Czechoslovakia.[16]

The previous evening, Kádár and Dubček met on the Hungarian–Czechoslovak border at Komárno. During this interview, Kádár tried to determine whether Dubček was willing to make a radical change in Czechoslovak policy under outside pressure.[17] Believing that this was not the case, he finally gave his agreement for the intervention.

The CPSU Politburo meeting on 17 August marked the final step in the preparation of the invasion. Brezhnev explained that Dubček was disoriented and that the next KSČ Congress would see the triumph of "right-wingers". He announced that elements of the KSČ leadership had prepared a plan and requested a military intervention on 21 August.[18] The Politburo decided to "adopt active measures to save socialism in Czechoslovakia and decided unanimously to provide the Communist Party and the peoples of Czechoslovakia with assistance and support from the armed forces". Assured of the support and participation of the WTO countries, Brezhnev finally gave the order to launch Operation Danube.[19]

A meeting of the leaders of the WTO countries whose troops were to take part in the military operation took place on 18 August to endorse Brezhnev's decision. Kádár reported that discussions with Dubček were sterile. The report of the Hungarian leader was followed by the ratification of the Soviet decision to implement an intervention in Czechoslovakia and refine the preparations.

On the morning of 18 August, Grechko, who had just inspected Soviet, Polish and East German divisions, gathered 17 leading representatives of the Soviet Army and commanders of the WTO armies. Leaving directly from the Politburo meeting, he informed them of Brezhnev's agreement to the "introduction of Warsaw Pact armies into Czechoslovakia".[20]

After Grechkov's opening speech, Matveî Zakharov, Chief of the General Staff of the Soviet Armed Forces, presented a map of Czechoslovakia. General Kozanov, whose troops were in the south of the GDR, had to move quickly from north to south, close the western border with four divisions, keeping two divisions in reserve and to control western Bohemia, most of northern Bohemia and the southwestern part of central Bohemia. General Velichko, whose departure area was in southeast GDR, would join with two of his best divisions at Prague-Ruzyně Airport to support the 7th Guards Airborne Division. He was also responsible for the occupation of the northern and central regions of Bohemia along the Děčín–Ústí nad Labem–Litoměřice–Prague road. General Mayorov, whose starting point was in southwestern Ukraine and southern Poland, was due to open operations with the goal of dominating all of Slovakia and northern and southern Moravia. Grechko was careful to stress that the fate of Europe and the distribution of forces around the world depended on the determination of these three commanders.

Marshal Krylov then reported that anti-aircraft forces were ready, while Air Force Marshal Konstantin Vershinin confirmed the Air Force crews were also primed to go into action. Admiral Gorskov said the entire Soviet Navy was in a state of increased alertness, nuclear submarines were in a combat position and the Naval Air Force was capable of launching fighting operations within two hours. General Margelov reported on the preparation of the airborne divisions and cooperation with the Military Transport Administration.

The GSFG commander, Marshal Koshevoy, then assured that he had taken the necessary measures to deal with a possible reaction by NATO forces. The Southern Group of Forces commander, General Provalov, was more concise, as was the commander of the Northern Group of Forces in Poland, Skadov, who both indicated that final preparations were complete. General Yepishev then briefly reviewed the lengthy political and moral preparation of the troops. He said that the time had come to bring troops into Czechoslovakia, with D-day set for 20 August and H-hour at 2300 hours.[21]

It seems that it was at this meeting that the direct participation of the NVA in the invasion was ruled out. In July, however, the Soviets had instructed them to march on Karlovy Vary, Pilsen, Děčín and Ústí nad Labem, but at the meeting of 18 August these missions were not mentioned. Indeed, the Czechoslovak conservatives had indicated their opposition to the military participation of East Berlin.[22] It was also during this meeting that the USSR General Secretary of Defence, Marshal Pavlovsky, was appointed commander of the intervention forces and left, on Grechko's orders, for the HQ of the Soviet Northern Group of Forces at Legnica in Poland, where he took command of Operation Danube.[23]

On 19 August, Provalov put on alert the Soviet 48th Motorised Rifle Division while the Hungarians mobilised the 8th Motorised Rifle Division, their anti-aircraft forces and set aside the 15th Motorised Rifle Division and the 24th and 35th Reconnaissance Battalions. In Sofia, Defence Minister Dobri Djurov and CoS General Atanas Semerjijev signed a decree authorising Bulgarian troops already in Ukraine under Soviet command to enter Czechoslovakia.[24]

Soviet paratroopers spent the day studying maps of Prague and films showing many views of the streets, bridges over the Vltava River and administrative buildings, learning to navigate easily around an unknown city. On the same day, the 3rd, 12th and 112th Military Transport Aviation Regiments prepared 440 AN-12s to participate in the invasion. On the ground, soldiers from the units participating in Operation Danube moved from the cities to their places of concentration in the forests. For the Czech intelligence services, it was a clear sign that something was happening but the inhabitants of Czechoslovakia did not know anything about it. A bulletin of the Czechoslovak Ministry of the Interior ended with the following declaration: "Otherwise, the whole territory of Czechoslovakia is calm and there are no major events of political importance."[25]

Overthrow Dubček

Operation Danube was only the military side of a global strategy that also had a political component. According to Brezhnev, Czechoslovak opponents to Dubček had to guarantee the political legality of the intervention and provide a new direction for the KSČ and the government by overthrowing the reformist leadership. The connection between them and the Kremlin was via the Soviet embassy, and it was through this channel that Moscow gave their instructions. Dubček's opponents were meeting from 16–18 August at the Central Committee recreation centre in Orlík to discuss a memorandum of political support for military intervention. Central Committee conservative Indra then visited Chervonenko, who forwarded the document to Brezhnev. The ambassador received in return the order from Moscow to give Biľak and Indra a draft declaration to be sent to the citizens of Czechoslovakia after the start of the invasion. He also confirmed his agreement with a letter asking for assistance and promised to help them quickly. Moscow hesitated only as to when to launch the operation: either 20 August, at the time of the KSČ Presidium meeting, or the 26th, at the opening of the KSS Congress. The Czechs chose the date of the 20th.[26]

On 19 August, the Soviets confirmed the date of entry of WTO troops into Czechoslovakia as the night of 20-21 August. At that moment, the conservatives were to trigger a political crisis by imposing a debate on the letters sent by Brezhnev and the Soviet Politburo to Dubček on the violation of the Čierna agreement and that Dubček did not make public. The debate would culminate with the adoption of a resolution condemning the reformers and a seizure of power that would then be supported by WTO armed forces. On the morning of 21 August, a second 'letter of invitation' was to be issued, calling on fellow Warsaw Pact countries to intervene to save the country. In addition to the 11 signatories of the first letter, Indra also needed to receive 50 additional signatures from members of the KSČ Central Committee and government. He had to rely on the support of leaders close to Dubček. On the morning of 21 August, the printers and editors of *Rudé Právo* were to publish the letter, while Karel Hoffmann, director of the Central Communications Service, was to shut down all means of communication, namely radio and television, telegraph and telephone networks.

According to this plan, a group of conservatives would then go on radio and television and explain the situation to the public. From 21-22 August, a session of the KSČ Central Committee and a meeting of the National Assembly would be convened to endorse the overthrow of the Dubček administration and to request further military assistance from the WTO. In order to ensure the smooth operation of the KSČ apparatus at all levels, the conservatives established a list of leaders and loyal executives and a list of 20–30 journalists who would be responsible for informing the population. The post of Prime Minister of the new government was to be offered to Černík, and in case of refusal, a provisional government would be formed.[27]

The Soviets could also count on the support of leaders of the Czechoslovak security forces, including Viliam Šalgovič, who worked closely with the State Police's Colonel Nazarov, StB representative within the KGB, and General Mikhail Grigorievich Kotov, KGB representative in the Czechoslovak Interior Ministry. The KGB leader, Yuri Andropov, who had been stationed in Budapest in 1956, was a strong supporter of the intervention, which he had been calling for since Dubček came to power. In order to take active action in Prague, the KGB quickly installed agents unknown to Czechoslovak authorities. They were ordered to join organisations deemed 'counter-revolutionary', such as Club 231 and the Social Democratic Party, and the state television or the university, to obtain information on the reformers and to discredit them. The KGB also provided the StB with fictitious reports on the activities of KAN and Club 231 and their links with Western intelligence services.

The plan to overthrow Dubček was implemented from 18 August when the Interior Ministry was put on alert. Šalgovič, Lieutenant-Colonel Ripl and Colonel Dudáš sat down at a table in the main administration building of the StB with Soviet KGB advisers led by General Kotov. During the meeting, they planned and prepared both the WTO military intervention and the overthrow of Dubček. Šalgovič gave instructions to secure television and radio installations, protect the State Security Building on Sadová Street, secure Prague airport and stop transport by air.[28]

The regional chiefs of the National Security Corps (Sbor národní bezpečnost, or SNB) were also ordered by telex to declare the state of readiness to all officers, to take control of television and radio transmitters and post offices, and contact the media, to ensure that only acceptable emissions were broadcast. They also had to make sure that the SNB's buildings were secure.[29] Meanwhile, a group of 'Soviet

The enforced removal of General Václav Prchlík (centre, with cap), in July 1968, made sure that the ČSLA would not resist a military intervention of the WTO.

tourists' arrived at the Soviet embassy in Prague; among them were KGB agents.[30]

On 19 August, Dubček's opponents continued their arrangements. Karel Hoffmann oversaw preparations for the release of the Central Communication Administration building with the help of StB agents.[31] In Sadová Street, at StB headquarters – under the leadership of General Kotov – Šalgovič and Ripl mobilised border guards and dozens of State Security personnel to facilitate the invasion of the country.

The conservatives' political overthrow of Dubček was intended to help prevent the ČSLA's resistance to the invasion. This question was crucial, because Danube Operation still appeared a risky proposition. Czechoslovak territory was easy to defend, especially since Prague had nothing to fear from the FRG and Austria, and Hungary only reluctantly participated in the operation. The danger therefore came mainly from the USSR, Poland and the GDR. By simply blocking a dozen roads they could stop an armoured invasion, while defending a small number of air bases would make a rapid invasion impossible.

To avoid such a disastrous scenario, the Soviets were in direct contact with the ČSLA command through General Yamschikov, the WTO representative in Prague. They had already obtained an advantage by causing the resignation of General Václav Prchlík in mid-July. At a press conference on 15 July, Prchlík criticised the WTO, provoking protests by the Soviets, who accused him of having disclosed military secrets. To avoid scandal, Prchlík was fired.[32] The real reason for his 'elimination', besides Prchlík being a staunch supporter of the reforms, was probably that he was the only military man to consider armed resistance against a possible Soviet invasion, a matter he had spoken about with Dubček on 24 July.[33]

Late on the afternoon of 20 August, General Kodaj, commander of the Czechoslovak Eastern Military District, learnt that Hungarian units were concentrated near the border. Dzúr, the Defence Minister, was informed, but around 2200 hours, when he received a call from Černík asking if the borders with Hungary and Poland were calm, he answered that they were. Then, with Šalgovič, he went to General Yamschikov's apartment, where Soviet Ambassador Chervonenko was waiting for him with the KGB's Colonel Petr Ivanovich Kambulov.[34]

According to General Pavlovsky, Brezhnev and Grechko then called Dzúr to inform him of the imminent invasion and request that the ČSLA did not resist. They warned him that if the ČSLA did not cooperate, the Soviets were ready to use force to liquidate the counter-revolution in Czechoslovakia. More directly and brutally, Grechko threatened "to hang him personally to the nearest tree if he fires a single shot against the Soviet troops".[35] Dzúr duly promised the ČSLA would not oppose the invasion. He went to the Staff building, where a Military Council had already been prepared. At this meeting, which began after 2300 hours, Dzúr informed the participants that WTO armies had entered Czechoslovakia and the ČSLA would not resist them. He added that the KSČ and State leaderships also agreed with this position. Around midnight, with the approval of the Military Council, he ordered all ČSLA forces to remain in their barracks, not to use their weapons and to provide assistance when requested by the WTO troops. This order, according to the instructions of Moscow, had been prepared with General Yamschikov.[36]

Shortly after midnight, the order was given to the commander of the ČSLA's 10th Air Army and the 7th Air Defence Force to prohibit all Air Force aircraft from taking off, to ensure the landing of Soviet aircraft at Brno and Ruzyně-Prague Airport, to refuse the use of weapons and to assist the Warsaw Pact troops.[37] During the previous afternoon, Lieutenant Colonel Ripl had alerted the 25 members of the

Upon receiving direct threats to his life, General Martin Dzúr, the Defence Minister of Czechoslovakia and a moderate reformer close to Dubček, decided that the ČSLA would not resist the invasion. Awarded for this decision, he was to retain his position until 1985. (MOD Czech Republic)

border control at Ruzyně Airport of the imminence of a "night event". Shortly after 2330 hours, instructions were finally given to them:

> By order of the President of the Republic and with the approval of the KSČ and the Government, the armies of the Warsaw Pact States [will] occupy Czechoslovakia. Ensure the smooth landing of aircraft and their crews. In case of resistance by civilian personnel, use weapons.[38]

General Yamschikov perfectly fulfilled the mission entrusted to him by the Kremlin. The ČSLA commanders were summoned around 2300 hours to learn of the entry of WTO troops and to receive orders from the Defence Minister. Thanks to these orders issued by the ČSLA Staff, Moscow ensured the neutralisation of the Czechoslovak armed forces.

The failure of the political coup

It was with increasing nervousness that preparations for the conservatives' political coup continued. On the morning of 20 August, members of the KSČ Presidium and Secretariat prepared for a meeting that was originally scheduled to take place at 1000 hours but was postponed until 1400 hours. It was to be devoted to preparations for the 14th KSČ Congress.

Throughout the morning, Biľak, Indra and Kolder tried to rally other leaders to their conspiracy and to make them sign the letter asking for the WTO's help. Kolder tried to convince Černík and Kolar, but without success. Lenárt, who had probably planned what was going to happen, preferred to report sick and was hospitalised. The conservatives quickly realised they were politically isolated and still in the minority.[39]

Faced with the actions of their opponents, Dubček's supporters did not remain inactive. Josef Spacek met Dubček in his apartment in the morning, and the two men agreed to block the moves of Indra and Kolder. KSČ Secretary Císař informed all the media, newspaper editors and radio and television stations that if the conservatives

By the time of the final act in the political struggle pro and contra a military intervention of the WTO, all the involved forces were already in place and ready to roll into Czechoslovakia. This photograph shows a T-54 and a BTR-152 of an unknown Soviet motorised rifle unit, both already 'decorated' with vertical white identification stripes down their fronts and sides – waiting for the signal to move.

overthrew Dubček at the Central Committee meeting, they should be ready to let Dubček broadcast quickly, while the reformers stood ready to organise mass rallies in the capital.

As expected, the conservatives went on the offensive early on at the Presidium meeting. Kolder demanded that Brezhnev's letter on the country's situation be discussed first. With Emil Rigo and Biľak, he wanted to start a debate that was supposed to disrupt the meeting and push it to take concrete measures. Kolder's speech was followed by a lively discussion. But the conservatives did not receive enough support, and their proposal for debate was postponed to discuss Dubček's speech for the next KSČ Congress. The debate on Dubček's speech lasted until 2300 hours, after which the conservatives asked again to discuss their proposal for a debate on a political situation they considered to be counter-revolutionary. This new proposal, while supported by Biľak, Kapek and Rigo, was rejected by the rest of the Presidium.[40]

Shortly after 2300 hours, Colonel Hošek informed Černík of the crossing of the border by WTO troops. Immediately after, Dzúr confirmed this message by telephone. Talks continued in the Presidium until, just after 2330 hours, Černík arrived to announce the start of the invasion.[41] Zdeněk Mlynář immediately reacted, stating: "I am the secretary of the Central Committee of the Communist Party. I will not be secretary in an occupied country." The conservatives were surprised by the early start of the intervention, since they were not yet able to take control of the country without a majority in the Presidium. Dubček took the floor and said that what was happening was done without the knowledge of the Prime Minister, the President of the National Assembly, the President of the Republic and the KSČ General Secretary.[42]

Before midnight on 20 August, the Soviet Ambassador, accompanied by KGB General Kambulov, asked to be admitted to President Svoboda to announce to him, on behalf of the heads of state of the USSR and the other countries involved, the entry of their troops into the country to fight against the danger of a counter-revolution. Svoboda was not surprised, since during the day his ambassador in Hungary had sent a telegram to inform him of an anonymous phone call to a ČTK journalist[43] in Budapest announcing that the invasion of his country would begin at midnight.[44] The Soviet ambassador asked Svoboda to give a reassuring speech to the population and gave him a prepared text. The Czechoslovakian President said he would not welcome WTO troops but would do everything in his power to prevent resistance and bloodshed.[45]

Shortly after, Svoboda and Interior Minister Josef Pavel arrived at the Presidium meeting, where discussions continued. The President took the floor to announce that around midnight, Ambassador Chervonenko had visited him to warn of the beginning of the invasion. He stressed that everything had to be done to avoid bloodshed. After a brief silence, Smrkovský asked: "What will we say to the nation?" Dubček proposed the drafting of a statement that would be circulated by the government to prevent false information from reaching the media. The statement was written by Václav Slavík, Čestmír Císař and Mlynář, but Biľak and Kolder protested against some of the wording, which they believed could provoke hostility from the Soviets. The text was finally voted for by Dubček, Černík, Smrkovský, Barbírek, Kriegel, Piller and Spacek, with Biľak and Kolder voting against it, while Rigo and Švestka approved its contents but asked for changes in the wording. Following its approval, the statement was faxed to the KSČ District and Regional Committees, the KSS Central Committee and the media.[46]

At 0200 hours, Bohumil Šimon, the head of the KSČ in Prague, went to the Central Committee building, where he suggested to Dubček that he convene a meeting of the elected delegates to the 14th Congress, and to prepare a general strike and an appeal to the communist parties of the world.[47] Kolder, Biľak and Indra, finally vanquished, sought refuge at the Soviet embassy,[48] while Švestka went to the headquarters of *Rude Pravo*, Piller to the central Bohemian region and Černík to the government building. Dubček, Kriegel, Smrkovský, Spacek, Mlynář, Slavik, Sadovsky and Simon stayed in the Central Committee meeting room, and others went to their offices without leaving the building.

The statement of the KSČ Presidium condemning the invasion was transmitted by radio to the population around 0200 hours. Despite the fact that the speaker's voice was briefly silenced when it was broadcast – Hoffmann shutting down the transmitter – the statement was broadcast across the country and around the world. It condemned the military intervention but asked that it not be resisted by force. Above all, it asserted that the state and KSČ leaders remained in place. This statement played a key role in the coming days, especially in the emergence of civil resistance against the invasion. Above all, it signalled the failure of the political component of Operation Danube, whose success now depended only on its military component.[49]

6

THE INVASION

Within the first few hours of 21 August 1968, hundreds of thousands of soldiers and thousands of tanks and armoured vehicles swept over Czechoslovakia. Operation Danube demonstrated the Soviets' perfect command of large-scale military operations, especially as it was not only a land operation but also an airborne and aerial one. It marked the end of the Prague Spring.

Invasion forces

The WTO forces participating in the invasion of Czechoslovakia were grouped into three operational Fronts. The most important was the Carpathian Front, commanded by General Vasily Bisyarin, whose troops were largely concentrated in the area of Legnica-Krakow in Poland. It included the Polish 2nd Army (4th Motorised Rifle Division and 10th and 11th Tank Divisions) and the Polish 6th Airborne Division. The Polish headquarters was located in Swidnica, while the 11th Tank Division was in Javor, the 10th Tank Division in the Opole region and the 4th Motorised Rifle Division south of Swidnica, only a few kilometres from the Czechoslovak border.

On the right flank of the Poles was the Soviet 11th Army (1st and 18th Guards Motorised Rifle Divisions, and 20th Tank Division). The 20th Motorised Rifle Division, commanded by Major General Ivan Zhebrunov, covered the rear of the 90th Guards Motorised Rifle Division of the Norther Group of Forces and next to it, on the border of the GDR and Poland, was the 18th Guards Motorised Rifle Division. The 1st Guards Motorised Rifle Division was deployed in the GDR in the area of Cottbus–Juterbog, where it remained in reserve for the 18th Guards Motorised Rifle Division.[1]

The last component of the Carpathian Front was formed by the Soviet 38th Army, commanded by General Mayorov. It now had two tank divisions, the 15th Guards under Major General Zaitsev and the 31st (Major General Yourkov), and four motorised rifle divisions (the 24th, 30th, 48th and 128th Guards). The 15th Tank Division, commanded by Major General Zaitsev, formerly part of the 28th Army of the Belarussian Military District, was redeployed to Transcarpathia. Major General Yurkov's 31st Tank Division was from the 8th Tank Army of the Carpathian Military District, while the 48th Motorised Rifle Division arrived from the Odessa Military District.[2]

To invade Czechoslovakia from the east and occupy Slovakia, the 31st Motorised Rifle Division had to advance through Michalovce towards Trenčín and the 128th Motorised Rifle Division from Kosice to Banska Bystrica. After a march of approximately 500km to the west, they were to join the 24th Motorised Rifle Division, occupying Ostrava in the north, and the 254th Motorised Rifle Division in the south near Brno. The Carpathian Front was supported by the 4th and 9th Air Armies.

From the Klingental-Dresden region in the GDR, the Central Front was concentrating with GSFG troops commanded by General Shkadov. It included the 1st Guards Tank Army under the command of General Kozhanov (6th, 14th, 20th, 23rd and 35th Guards Motorised Rifle Divisions, and 9th and 11th Tank Divisions), the 20th Guards Army under General Velichko (9th and 11th Tank Divisions and 20th Guards Motorised Rifle Division) and the 27th Guards Motorised Rifle Division of the Soviet 8th Army. These forces were supported by the 16th and 24th Air Armies.[3]

As far as GDR troops were concerned, the NVA 7th Armoured Division was waiting in the Nochten sector and the 11th Motorised Rifle Division was concentrated in the area of Eisenberg–Jena–Neustadt–Gera. These forces remained in reserve on GDR territory. Only a few units of the NVA's 12th Border Patrol Regiment, who secured the border, were to enter Czechoslovakia, as well as intelligence, reconnaissance and liaison groups accompanying the main Soviet army officers. Within the HQ of the invading armies in Milovice, an operational group of several officers and six East German non-commissioned officers worked in liaison with the NVA High Command and provided 13 radio operators of the 2nd Liaison Regiment who moved with the Soviets from Legnica to Milovice on 23 August.[4]

The Southern Front under the command of General Provalov was in Hungary and included Soviet forces of the Southern Group of Forces, with the 13th Guards Tank Division (27th, 106th and 201st Guards Tank Regiments, 15th Tank Regiment and 78th Guards Motorised Rifle Regiment), the 254th Motorised Rifle Division (66th Tank Regiment and 95th, 96th and 97th Motorised Rifle Regiments), the 93rd Guards Motorised Rifle Division (59th

A poor, but very interesting photograph of an armoured recovery and supply vehicle based on the chassis of the SU-152 or ISU-152 heavy assault gun, with a large container for spare gun barrels on the roof, approaching the border of Czechoslovakia, late on 20 August 1968. Notably, the identification stripe on its front was applied crudely over spare tracks and towing winches.

Table 3: WTO ground units participating in Operation Danube (Clockwise)		
Overall Commander		Marshal Ivan Pavlovsky (USSR)
Directly Subordinated		
	7th Guards Airborne Division	General Lev Gorelov
	103rd Guards Airborne Division	General Alexander Yatsenko
Central Front	Klingental-Dresden region, GDR	General Ivan Shkadov
1st Guards Tank Army (USSR)	9th Tank Division	
	11th Tank Division	
	6th Guards Motorised Rifle Division	
	14th Guards Motorised Rifle Division	
	20th Guards Motorised Rifle Division	
	23rd Guards Motorised Rifle Division	
	35th Guards Motorised Rifle Division	
20th Guards Army (USSR)	9th Tank Division	General Ivan Velichko
	11th Tank Division	
	20th Guards Motorised Rifle Division	
	27th Guards Motorised Rifle Division	
	7th Panzer-Division (NVA)	Nochten region, held in reserve
	11th Motorised Rifle Division (NVA)	Neustadt-Gera region, held in reserve
	12th Border Patrol Regiment (NVA)	
Carpathian Front	Legnica-Krakow region, Poland	General Vasily Bisyarin
11th Army (USSR)	1st Guards Motorised Rifle Division	Cottbus-Juterborg region, held as reserve
	18th Guards Motorised Rifle Division	
	20th Tank Division	
	20th Motorised Rifle Division	General Ivan Zhebrunov, held as reserve
	90th Guards Motorised Rifle Division	
2nd Army (Poland)	4th Motorised Rifle Division	Swidnica region
	6th Airborne Division	
	10th Tank Division	Opole region
	11th Tank Division	Javor region
38th Army (USSR)	15th Guards Tank Division	General Mikhail Zaitsev
	31st Guards Tank Division	General Yourkov
	24th Motorised Rifle Division	
	30th Motorised Rifle Division	
	48th Motorised Rifle Division	
	128th Guards Motorised Rifle Division	
	12th Motorised Rifle Regiment (Bulgaria)	
	25th Motorised Rifle Regiment (Bulgaria)	
Southern Front (USSR)	Hungary	General Konstantin Provalov
	13th Guards Tank Division	
	48th Motorised Rifle Division	
	93rd Guards Motorised Rifle Division	
	254th Motorised Rifle Division	
	8th Motorised Rifle Division (Hungary)	

Guards Tank Regiment and 110th, 111th and 112th Guards Motorised Rifle Regiments) and the 48th Motorised Rifle Division (10th Guards Tank Regiment, 375th Tank Regiment, 265th Guards Motorised Rifle Regiment and 330th and 333rd Motorised Rifle Regiments). The 36th Air Army provided air support. The Hungarians took part with their 8th Motorised Rifle Division and some Air Force units concentrated at the air bases of Taszar, Papa and Kecskemét. On the evening of 20 August, ammunition was provided to the units that were taking part in the invasion.[5]

In order to avoid misunderstandings and possible incidents of 'friendly fire', white stripes were painted on WTO combat and transport vehicles involved, with two vertical red stripes on aircraft.[6] All vehicles without these bands were to be "neutralised", preferably "without firing". In case of resistance, they were to be "immediately destroyed". In the unlikely event of contact with NATO forces, WTO troops were ordered to stop immediately and "not fire without order".[7]

Operation Danube assigned a crucial role to the Soviet Airborne Forces (Vozdushno-desantnye voyska, VDV): the 103rd Guards Airborne Division of Colonel Alexander Yatsenko and the 7th Guards Airborne Division under Major General Lev Gorelov. For their landing on the Czechoslovak airfields, the Military Transport Aviation mobilised 440 AN-12s. The 103rd Guards Airborne Division's protection was ensured by two fighter regiments and a fighter-bomber regiment of the 36th Air Army. The Náměšť nad Oslavou Air Base and Brno-Turany Airport were thus permanently overflown at an altitude of 2,000–3,000 metres by four fighter-jets.

In addition, 16 fighter-bombers were on alert to attack four positions of the Czechoslovak anti-aircraft missile divisions. Coverage for the 7th Guards Airborne Division was provided by the 16th Air Army with between four and eight fighter-jets flying at an altitude of 800–2,000 metres over the landing areas. If necessary, the forces of two fighter-bomber regiments would attack Czechoslovak anti-aircraft missile positions.[8]

The WTO countries never revealed the total number of soldiers and military equipment deployed for Operation Danube. At a meeting of the Czechoslovak National Assembly held on 26 August 1968, General Rusov, the ČSLA CoS, estimated that there were 12 tank divisions, 13 motorised rifle divisions and two airborne divisions, with some 6,300 T-62, T-55, T-54 and T-34 tanks, 2,000 guns and an aerial force of 550 fighter aircraft and 250 transport aircraft. Official figures for WTO forces on Czechoslovak territory were only known for the Southern Front: 48,055 soldiers, 840 tanks, 694 armoured vehicles, 7,253 other vehicles and 177 aircraft and helicopters. The invasion thus mobilised 27 divisions with about 300,000 soldiers, but their number could be increased to more than half a million within a few days, and even as many as 800,000 troops with 2,000 guns, 7,500 tanks and 1,000 aircraft.[9]

To preserve the secrecy of Operation Danube and avoid leaks of information, preparations for combat were only carried out belatedly. Orders were also given to conceal troop departure areas and prevent unauthorised access to units and equipment. The precise content of the missions was only distributed to the commanders of the units, battalions and divisions on 19 August, and to all the soldiers on 20 August at 1700 hours, when the ammunition was handed over.[10]

At 2215 hours, the HQ in Legnica, where Marshal Yakubovsky was located, gave the starting signal for the operation by sending the codeword 'VLTAVA' to all the involved HQs. At 2300 hours, all units were put on alert via a closed-circuit communication channel, and a 'go' order was passed to all the fronts, armies, divisions, brigades, regiments and battalions.

Table 4: V-VS Units participating in Operation Danube[11]	
16th Air Army	GSFG (GDR)
4th Air Army	Northern Group of Forces (Poland)
36th Air Army	Southern Group of Forces (Hungary)
14th Air Army	Carpathian Military District
17th Air Army	Kiev Military District
1st Air Army	Byelorussian Military District

The capture of Prague

While in the hours preceding the invasion, the mass of involved ground troops remained in place, small reconnaissance groups set off along the border to help the rest of the invading forces to orient themselves. Other reconnaissance forces had the task of securing vital communication links. Officially at least, the involved units set in motion around 2200 hours. However, it was only shortly after 2100 hours when soldiers from the 56th Construction Battalion of the

The weather was anything but perfect during the late afternoon of 20 August 1968, when this photograph was taken of an An-12 transport waiting for Soviet VDV troops. It worsened during the following night: nevertheless, there was no way back and the aircraft hauling troops of the 7th and 103rd Guards Airborne Divisions went into action.

ČSLA reported two T-55 tanks and two personnel carriers of the NVA in Vejprty and saw East German reconnaissance patrols in Doupov and Nejdek. At 2300 hours, military columns crossing the border at Boží Dar, Cínovec, Černý Potok, Hranice, Luby and Nejdek left no doubt to the Czechoslovak authorities of the reality of the invasion.[12]

The NVA's early participation did not risk Operation Danube, because Soviet forces had already entered Czechoslovakia.[13] Shortly after 2100 hours, the BND's listening centre located in Pullach, near Munich, realised that total radio silence had been imposed upon Prague-Ruzyně International Airport.[14] This marked the beginning of the airborne phase of Operation Danube. The 7th Guards Airborne Division was to seize the airports at Prague, Kbely, Vodochody and the largest one in Ruzyně. Some of the paratroopers were to go to the capital, while the others stayed in the occupied airports until the arrival of the Bulgarian 22nd Motorised Rifle Regiment. The 103rd Guards Airborne Division was to take control of Brno-Tuřany Airport and the Náměš nad Oslavou Air Base.[15]

At 2050 hours, a civilian AN-12 from Moscow landed at Prague-Ruzyně Airport and parked on the tarmac reserved for Aeroflot. It was equipped with a guidance device for landing. About an hour later, an Il-14 from Lvov landed there, carrying a group of about 25 civilians, headed by the head of Aeroflot's subsidiary in Prague and KGB member Makarov. After meeting with ČSLA officials, they got into cars and headed for the Czechoslovak capital.[16]

Meanwhile, at 2130 hours, Marshal Grechko ordered the 7th and 103rd Guards Airborne Divisions into action. Half an hour later, the two divisions were ready for combat; at 2330 hours, an assault group from the 108th Airborne Regiment took off to take control of Ruzyně Airport, while Marshal Skripko, commander of the Transport Military Administration, ordered the paratroopers of the 7th Guards Airborne Division to embark, even though the weather was far from

One of the An-12s used to deploy troops of the 7th Guards Airborne Division seen on the tarmac of Ruzyně Airport, together with one of the MiG-21UMs that escorted it there, early on 21 August 1968.

An-12s on the ground at Ruzyně, together with a Praga 37mm anti-aircraft cannon of the ČSLA, the crew of which obviously sided with the invaders.

Mi-6s of the 688th Independent Helicopter Regiment underway into Czechoslovakia, on the morning of 21 August 1968.

ideal, a storm and rain forcing their aircraft to fly at an altitude of 4,000 metres.[17]

Shortly after 2300 hours, Pullach radars were blinded by Soviet ground jammers. The operation involved two squadrons of six Tu-16P jamming aircraft from the 226th Heavy Bomber Aviation Regiment operating from Stryi Airport in Ukraine.[18] At least four other regiments with Il-28 and Yak-28 radio-electronic combat aircraft alternated in the air over Hungary (36th Soviet Air Army), the GDR (16th Air Army), Poland (4th Air Army) and the USSR (14th Air Army). They

An Mi-4 of the 688th Independent Helicopter Regiment approaching Ruzyně Airport. While obviously wearing the standard camouflage pattern consisting of dark green on upper surfaces and sides, and light admiralty grey on undersides, 'Yellow 36' also received two red identification strips around its boom.

were coordinated by the 67th Independent Radar Tracking Squadron using a Tu-126 radar aircraft named LIANA. The latter could also locate signals indicating the possible take-off of Czechoslovak aircraft. If this happened, the Czechs would face about 100 Soviet MiG-21 or MiG-19 fighter-jets.[19]

Consequently, ČSLA radars could not spot dozens of An-12s – escorted by two regiments of fighters and two of fighter-bombers of the 16th Air Army – that carried the first wave of paratroopers to Ruzyně. The first An-12 landed on runway 25 still fully lit, carrying the command of the 7th Guards Airborne Division: this unit took control of the main buildings of the airport within 15 minutes. At 30-second intervals, the other An-12s landed, and the parachutists disembarked from each aircraft within two or three minutes. Empty aircraft took off again on Runway 13, heading for Belarus to embark reinforcements.[20] During the day, Mi-6 and Mi-4 helicopters of the 688th Independent Helicopter Regiment – with its main base in Legnica, Poland – carried mainly military equipment, ammunition, food and, in many cases, BTR-152 armoured personnel carriers.[21]

Immediately after regrouping, the Soviet paratroopers moved towards the centre of Prague, where only a few hours after touching down they were to take control of the governmental and military buildings, media headquarters and four bridges across the Vltava River, and ensure the protection of the Soviet embassy. The commander of the 7th Guards Airborne Division, Gorelov, had never been to Prague before, but had closely studied a plan of the city. In addition, extensive training had been provided to the commanders of the four mobile units tasked with accomplishing the division's goal. They were preceded by cars driven by KGB agents and embassy staff, who guided them through Prague.

At 0400 hours, the 108th Airborne Regiment on the left bank of the Vltava was the first to take control of the ČSLA HQ in Djevice. At 0440 hours, a reconnaissance company reinforced by ASU-57 self-propelled guns and a platoon of SPG-9 anti-tank guns seized Prague Castle, the residence of the President of the Republic.[22]

A unit of the 108th Regiment with a battery of ASU-85s was deployed in front of the government building. A first platoon entered the main entrance of the building and blocked the other entrances, while the access routes were guarded by ASU-85s, a parachute platoon and an SPG-9 platoon. Another platoon disarmed security staff and disabled all telephone links by cutting the cables. At 0440 hours, the deputy commander of the 108th Regiment, Lieutenant Colonel Gordienko, and the commander of the 2nd Platoon, Tarabanov, accompanied by a group of soldiers, entered the room housing the government. The Czech politicians were all surprised by this development and Černík, with tears in his eyes, picked up a phone, but Gordienko ordered everyone to stay put and await further instructions. Within 15 minutes, KGB operatives arrived and began to 'filter' the government staff: some were sent "under protection" to the building's cellar, while others, including Černík, were taken to Ruzyně.[23]

Around 0500 hours, Prague residents gathered to try to enter the government building and free the ministers. However, the paratroopers, supported by the battery of self-propelled guns, prevented them from doing so, resorting to force. Stones and sticks were thrown

An ASU-57 of the 108th Airborne Regiment advancing into downtown Prague early on 21 August 1968. Notable is the application of the white identification stripe with a spray gun over the VDV insignia.

at the soldiers, while some demonstrators tried to take their weapons from them.[24]

Crowds carrying banners and flags began to gather in front of the KSČ Central Committee building. Shortly after 0500 hours, Soviet armoured personnel carriers (APCs) and tanks arrived in front of the building. Paratroopers with burgundy berets and striped vests, automatic weapons in hand,[25] emerged from the armoured vehicles. They quickly surrounded the building, despite the hostile crowd shouting anti-Soviet slogans. Some Czechs tried to disarm the paratroopers, who needed the help of a battery of self-propelled guns and an engineering company to restore order. Some of the paratroopers immediately entered the building, while others tried to disperse the crowds by firing a few shots, one of which hit a 20-year-old man in the head and killed him. Smrkovský, who observed the scene from a window, called Chervonenko to tell him that the spilled blood was on his hands.

The paratroopers, led by Colonel Sereguin, neutralised the Central Committee security service and cut the central office's cables. Lieutenant Colonel Shiskin and Lieutenant Pritalyuk, accompanied by several soldiers, entered an office containing 25 people, including Dubček, Kriegel, Smrkovský, Simon and Spacek. The troops raised their weapons, and when Dubček tried to speak, the colonel shouted: "Do not talk! Be calm! Do not speak Czech!" When Kriegel asked what the Soviet troops were doing, Shiskin replied that the Soviet people had come to protect socialism in Czechoslovakia and asked those present to stay calm. Dubček wanted to call Chervonenko, then Brezhnev, but a lieutenant showed him the phone was out of order. Smrkovský then went to a window and began to shout at the crowd to warn of their arrest, asking that they act to release them.

The commander of the 108th Regiment, Lieutenant Colonel Minigulov, arrived and announced to Dubček that the Soviet forces had come to help him quell the counter-revolutionary rebellion. Dubček replied that there was no counter-revolution, then bullets began to hit the windows. Minigulov asked Dubček to call the population not to resist the Soviet troops, but Dubček refused. Minigulov then received a call from Gorelov, who ordered him to drive Dubček to Ruzyně.

Hard on the heels of the ASU-57s, there followed the first ASU-85 assault guns, carrying additional VDV troops in a rather 'traditional' Soviet fashion. The VDV were considered an elite and the quick-reaction reserve of the Soviet forces: all were stationed inside the territory of the USSR in peacetime and, kept at a high state of alert, were chosen to spearhead any major operation.

A rear view at the same column of ASU-85s as it was stopped by the mass of civilians blocking the street in front of them. Notable are details of the insignia and different gear on the vehicle in the foreground.

When Dubček, Smrkovský, Kriegel and Špaček left the building, the other members of KSČ Central Committee remained calm. Dubček and Kriegel were secured in one BTR-50P APC, with Smrkovský and Spacek in another, still under the supervision of two Soviet officers.[26] Arriving at Ruzyně, they embarked in Soviet transport aircraft which took them to Uzhhorod in Ukraine. According to some sources, the prisoners made a stopover in Legnica before reaching Ukraine.[27] That evening, Černík and Šimon were also arrested.[28]

Around 0600 hours, a reconnaissance company reinforced by a battery of ASU-85s encircled the Klement Gottwald Military Academy. Meanwhile, the 7th Airborne Company stopped near the barracks of the Prašneho Operational Brigade, having sighted armed soldiers in the courtyard. The Soviet commander divided his company into two groups, which surprised and disarmed the guards at both entrances to

While trying to reach the Hlavní Nádraží radio station, troops of the 9th Airborne Company VDV encountered barricades consisting of buses: these were mercilessly pushed aside by their ASU-85s.

When the column approached the radio station, it found itself surrounded by thousands of civilians: as soon as the ASU-85s stopped, they found their way blocked by additional trucks and passenger buses.

From 0500–0600 hours, the 119th Airborne Regiment and an artillery regiment landed at Vodochody Airport, 15km northwest of Prague. The airport was brought under Soviet control after the landing of the first aircraft carrying the 9th Airborne Company.[31] The regiment immediately moved on to take important buildings on the right bank of the Vltava River. On the way, they crossed barricades of cars and trams, and between 0700 and 0800 hours, they occupied the post office, the telegraph and radio buildings, the Charles University, the Czechoslovak Academy of Sciences, the StB headquarters, the Hlavní Nádraží station, the State Bank and the television building, where two paratroopers were wounded in an exchange of fire.

When the paratroopers arrived in front of the radio station, they found the building surrounded by thousands of demonstrators who had built an improvised barricade. They were themselves almost encircled, having to fire into the air to clear and get around the barricade. The Soviets said that shots were then fired at them. They responded by opening fire themselves and attacking the building. An assault group crossed the main entrance, but found their access blocked. Several paratroopers went to the courtyard of a neighbouring house, where they climbed a 4-metre-high wall and got into the courtyard of the radio building. There, two sergeants managed to gain access through a window on the second floor. Only then did the Soviets enter the building through the main entrance. They seized the first and second floors, but they still need two hours to take the third floor, where the studios were continuing with their transmissions. They eventually stopped all radio broadcasts and ordered the staff to gather in the lobby and await further orders.[32]

the barracks. At the second entrance, the commander of the group of paratroopers told his men to take up combat positions, then he called the commander of the ČSLA troops and ordered him to gather his men in the courtyard without resistance. The airborne troops, aided by an SPG-9 battery, disarmed some 700 Czechoslovak soldiers.[29]

At 0700 hours, the Defence Ministry, where KGB officers blockaded General Dzúr and his deputies in their offices, was occupied by the 1st Engineering Company of the 143rd Battalion, while the 6th Company of the 2nd Airborne Battalion occupied the Interior Ministry building in Letná. Other units of paratroopers took control of the anti-aircraft defence building and some of the Vltava bridges.[30]

At around 0630 hours, the first units of the 6th and 35th Motorised Rifle Divisions of the Soviet 20th Guards Army arrived from the GDR, reaching the Ruzyně and Vodochody Airports and linking up with the paratroopers before helping them to complete their takeover of Prague.[33] During the afternoon, units of the 11th Tank Army from Poland joined the paratroopers.

When Czechoslovak civilians attempted to disarm the invading troops, Soviet officers felt forced to draw their firearms in response: several of them opened fire at the unarmed civilians around them.

Civilians reacted by setting on fire vehicles used to block the street – which in turn engulfed at least one of the Soviet ASU-85s. As far as is known, two Soviet paratroopers were wounded in this clash.

The Invasion of Bohemia

The 1st Guards Tank Army of General Kozanov and the 20th Guards Army had the task of occupying Bohemia. The invasion of the western part of this region was entrusted to the 1st Tank Army, which was to take control of the border with the FRG, while the main objective of the 20th Guards Army was Prague.

The 1st Guards Tank Army crossed the border at Boží Dar and Hranice in the Černý Potok valley at 2300 hours, moving on via Vejprty, Cínovec, Nejdek, Luby, Kraslice and Vojtanov.[34] Its progress, like that of other divisions participating in Operation Danube, followed a specific pattern. The reconnaissance and strike groups were the first to cross the border, moving quickly into the heart of Czechoslovakia, followed by units that had to reach the furthest goals without seeking combat, and finally those tasked with disarming the ČSLA and occupying territory.

The main axis of the 1st Guards Tank Army passed through Karlovy Vary to Pilsen, then from west to south to the FRG border, towards Rozvadov, Česká Kubice and Železná Ruda. On its left flank, it followed the roads passing through Hradiště and Jince, while the right flank passed Aš, Cheb, Mariánské Lázně and Planou to Tachov.

At 0050 hours, the Soviet tanks of the 65th Motorised Rifle Regiment entered Cheb, and by 0300 hours they controlled the whole city, leaving it later that morning to settle 5km to the northeast. From Klingenthal in the GDR, the 28th Tank Regiment crossed the border at Kraslice and reached Sokolov, where they stayed until around 1700 hours. At 1645 hours, units entered Dolní Žandov and Kynžvart. In this area, the most westerly territory of Czechoslovakia, during the evening of 21 August, the 20th Guards Motorised Rifle Division – which had set up its headquarters in Milíkov – occupied the axis between Cheb and Mariánské Lázně, with the 29th Motorised Rifle Regiment north of Tachova, a tank regiment north of Plana and the 67th and 242nd Motorised Rifle Regiments between Mariánské Lázně and Lázně Kynžvart and in the Františkovy Lázně region.[35]

Soviet troops arrived in Karlovy Vary around 0130 hours from Jelení, Horní Blatná and Boží Dar. At 0200 hours, Soviet officers arrived at the barracks of the 20th Motorised Rifle Division of the ČSLA, while their troops took up positions in the adjacent streets. At 0210 hours, the barracks of the 12th Battalion were occupied. The Soviets left the city around noon, some of the units moving towards the military training area of the ČSLA in Hradiště. It was also at this time that Soviet troops were seen passing along the Kyselka–Luka road and NVA troops along the road from Klášterec nad Ohří to Radonice.[36]

The Soviets appeared around 0520 hours to the north and southwest of Pilsen, near Třemošná, Kozolupy and Zbůch (about 6–10km from the city). The first tanks entered the city about an hour later. At 0720 hours, Soviet tanks and APCs arrived at the air base of the 5th Fighter Regiment and the 45th Reconnaissance Bomber Regiment southwest of the city and blocked the runway. A new column of tanks and APCs, accompanied by a general who was designated as commander of the city, arrived in Pilsen at about 0900 hours. The Soviets occupied the local military administration building, where the Soviet commander based himself. He summoned the commander of the Czech garrison, the chief of police and the KSČ secretary. The ČSLA units in the city

Ultimately, the VDV troops dispersed the mass of demonstrators in front of the Hlavní Nádraží radio station, and then occupied the building. As far as is known, two of the involved soldiers were injured in the clashes.

This bridge outside Karlovy Vary did not survive the passage of the T-54s from the Soviet 27th Motorised Rifle Division – in turn resulting in a nice view of the makeshift identification stripes applied to the vehicle.

Following a mad dash from the border with East Germany, the first units of the Soviet 20th Guards Army reached Prague by around 06.30hrs local time. Some of these were equipped with the then still relatively new T-62 main battle tanks, seen in this photograph.

were neutralised by 1000 hours, with first the barracks of the 19th Tank Battalion and then that of the 259th Anti-aircraft Artillery Brigade blockaded. During the day, all roads leading from Pilsen around the outskirts of the city were guarded by three or four tanks and APCs.[37] At 0900 hours, the 1st and 322nd Artillery Brigades occupied Strašice, between Pilsen and Prague. About an hour later, Soviet troops passed through Holýšov (23rd Tank Regiment), Domažlice (12th Motorised Rifle Regiment), Česká Kubica, Klatovy (11th Motorised Rifle Regiment) and Železná Ruda, where they occupied a defensive position on the border with Bavaria. During the morning, control of the frontier with the FRG was reinforced with the arrival of further Soviet tanks and APCs. By the end of the day, the forces of the 27th Motorised Rifle Division occupied the entire Karlovy Vary region, those of the 9th Tank Division the Pilsen region and those of the 11th Guards Tank Division the central portion of Bohemia.[38]

The 20th Guards Army entered Czechoslovakia via Hrensko and set off at full speed along main roads as far as Decin, Usti nad Labem, Litomerice, Terezin and Prague. Its right flank progressed through Chomutov and Most, then went through Teplice and Bílina to Louny, and on to Žatec, Rakovník and Slaný.

At 0045 hours, Soviet troops passed through Teplice, followed by Chomutov at 0150 hours and Bílina at 0200 hours. About an hour later, they occupied the air base at Bílina, where a group of 12 MiG-21PF/PFM fighter-jets from the 31st Guards Fighter Regiment from Falkenberg in the GDR and the 85th Guards Fighter Regiment arrived between 0600 and 0700 hours. At 0500 hours, the Soviets were in Podbořany and a battalion of 30 T-62 tanks was guarding all exits from the ČSLA barracks. At 1130 hours, nine Soviet tanks and APCs arrived in Beroun, led by Major Pesek, who met local representatives of the KSČ and the government at noon. The Soviet officer demanded the disarmament of a section of ČSLA artillery which was in the city. Czechoslovak officers refused, after which, thanks to the mediation of General Yamshchikov, Major Pesek backtracked.[39]

On the main axis of the 20th Guards Army, columns of tanks invested Děčín and Litoměřice at 0045 hours. The Litoměřice barracks were encircled, and the Soviets demanded that ČSLA troops ceased all contact with their superiors and did not leave the barracks. From 0100–0500 hours, several columns of tanks, APCs and other vehicles

VDV troops and their vehicles inside a hangar at Prague-Ruzyně airport.

A group photo of Soviet airborne troops in front of the main terminal of Prague-Ruzyně airport.

An interesting series of photographs showing elements of a Soviet motorised rifle division moving through a border town in northern Czechoslovakia. The spearhead consisted of three T-54/55 main battle tanks, all wearing white identification stripes down their hull fronts and turret sides. Notable is the amount of personal gear attached to the fuel drums at the rear of the hull.

The T-54/55s were followed by engineers, including this MTU-20 armoured bridge-layer, carrying a bridge of 20m length and capable of carrying vehicles of up to 50 tonnes.

Engineers were followed by additional T-55s. This column included tanks having two sets of markings applied on their turrets: one set included a white triangle applied directly on the turret side, probably left over from Exercise Šumava and partially removed; the other included small tactical numbers inside a white rhomboid, applied on a piece of canvas.

Finally, tanks were followed by various support elements, including this BM-24T artillery tractor, carrying the 240mm BM-24 multiple rocket launcher with 12 tubes. The BM-24T weighted around 15 tonnes and had a crew of six.

moved via Terezín, Bohušovice nad Ohří and in the direction of Prague in order to blockade ČSLA barracks in this area.[40]

The strategic goal for the 6th Guards Motorised Rifle Division (35th, 81st and 82nd Guards Motorised Rifle Regiments and 8th Guards Tank Regiment), the 14th Guards Motorised Rifle Division and the 35th Motorised Rifle Division was to reach Prague, where advanced units of the 6th Guards Motorised Rifle Division arrived at dawn to support the 7th Guards Airborne Division. At 0630 hours, the main units arrived at Ruzyně and Vodochody, where they divided into two columns and followed both banks of the Vltava River into Prague.[41]

WTO troops continued all day long to disembark at Prague's airports. Between 0700 and 0800 hours, a battery of the 97th Airborne Artillery Regiment landed in Ruzyně. They were followed later that day by the Bulgarian 22nd Motorised Rifle Regiment, which had taken off from Kolomyya in Ukraine. Its mission was to ensure the security of the airports of Vodochody and Ruzyně, assisted by Czechoslovakian border control officers under the command of the head of the Interior Ministry squadron, Colonel Eliáš.[42]

At 1300 hours, the 7th Guards Airborne Division passed under the command of the 20th Army, and the landing of the remainder of the division began at 1625 hours. At 1800 hours, the combat tasks of the division were declared fulfilled, although airborne patrols continued around Prague's most strategically important buildings.[43]

On the left wing of the 20th Army, the 18th Guards Motorised Rifle Division (360th Tank Regiment and 275th, 278th and 280th Motorised Rifle Regiments) of the 11th Guards Army left the Görlitz area in the direction of northern Bohemia along two axes, one from

Rumburk to Česká Lípa and the other via Liberec to Turnov. Around 0035 hours, the Soviets occupied Česká Lípa, where there was a base of the Czechoslovak 10th Air Army which was placed under control by around 0200 hours. The first AN-12 landed at this base around 0400 hours, followed by MiG-21PFM and Mi-6 helicopters. Soviet tank columns passed through Liberec at 0200 hours.

The 20th Tank Division (8th and 76th Guards Tank Regiments, 155th Tank Regiment and 144th Motorised Rifle Regiment) advanced from Sklarska Poreba in Poland through Harrachov, Turnov and Mnichovo Hradiste to Mlada Boleslav. Shortly before 0300 hours, Soviet troops entered Turnov, and Mladá Boleslav was occupied an hour later by a motorised rifle battalion reinforced by a tank company. A tank battalion led by the deputy commander of the 20th Army blocked all exits from the barracks and the city's airport. Some of the units then moved to Brandýs nad Labem and Stará Boleslav, 20km northeast of Prague, while others headed for the ČSLA training centre in Mladá.[44]

The Carpathian Front in Moravia

The invasion of eastern Bohemia and northern Moravia was entrusted to troops from Poland. The Polish 11th Tank Division, concentrated in a starting area between Lubawka and Mieroszów, was to move along two axes. The first followed the road from Lubawka to Tynec nad Labem and the second that from Mierozsow to Čáslav. The division was assisted in its progress by 13 Lim-2R reconnaissance aircraft and approximately two dozen Mi-2, Mi-4 and Mi-8T helicopters.[45]

The first mission of the Polish forces was to seize border crossing points and customs and frontier guard posts. This task was entrusted to the 1st Assault Battalion, which approached the designated targets while waiting to attack at the launch of Operation Danube. One of the groups of the 1st Assault Battalion, led by Lieutenant Jerzy Wróblem, seized the border building at Lubawka. The Czechoslovak border guards were all arrested. Polish forces did the same in Královec, Bernartice, Žacléř, Chvaleč and Trutnov. At 0120 hours, one of the assault groups led by Lieutenant Labuszewski seized the local television station at Černá Hora. Behind the assault groups came the Polish armoured vehicles, which moved through Trutnov and, at 0530 hours, Hořice.[46]

The columns of the Soviet and Polish armies invading northern Czechoslovakia were spearheaded by BRDM-1 armoured scout cars: indeed, their appearance was usually the first indication of incoming invaders.

Some tank units of the Soviet Army invading northern Czechoslovakia were still equipped with older T-10M heavy tanks. A top view of this example reveals a neat application of the white identification stripes across and down the turret, and the front and rear hull.

A poor quality but very interesting photograph of an armoured recovery vehicle based on the chassis of the IS-3 heavy tank crossing the border into Czechoslovakia. Relatively few such vehicles are known to have been used by the Polish Army of the 1960s.

OPERATION DANUBE: SOVIET AND WARSAW PACT INTERVENTION IN CZECHOSLOVAKIA, 1968

A Yak-28P of the Soviet air force, making a low-altitude, high-speed reconnaissance pass over Hradec Kralove on the morning of 21 August 1968. Notable is the application of two red identification stripes around the rear fuselage.

Troops of the Polish 25th Motorised Rifle Regiment run into barricades and protesting civilians in Olomouc, which forced them to stop and disembark their vehicles.

Barricades and clashes with protesting civilians in Olomuc also slowed down the advance of the next Polish unit, the 2nd Tank Regiment.

The Polish units progressed without major problems until dawn, but the Czech people became more numerous on the streets as the hours went by and started to pose a problem to the advance of the invading troops. Civilians demonstrated against the passage of troops, while others built barricades with cars, old trucks and sometimes even agricultural machinery to slow them down. In Trutnov, for example, a flaming tyre wall prevented the Poles from crossing the city for several hours. However, during the morning, the Poles finally reached Čáslav.

Between 0800 and 0900 hours, the air base at Čáslav was overflown by Soviet IL-28R reconnaissance aircraft, and the first MiG-15UTI SA landed around 0800 hours. Shortly after noon, another Soviet MiG-15UTI landed, followed by the arrival of 38 Soviet MiG-19S fighters from the 168th Fighter Aviation Division at Legnica. It was only during the afternoon that Polish armoured vehicles arrived at the entrance of the air base, but the Czechoslovak staff refused to let them enter. The 8th Tank Regiment, meanwhile, occupied Jičín, Městec Králové, Jičíněves, Slatiny, Liběšice, Kamenice and Kováč.[47]

On the second axis of the Polish 11th Tank Division, soldiers took Teplice nad Metují at 0045 hours after the frontier posts were neutralised, the garrisons of border guards and SNB being disarmed and some arrested. Some of the prisoners were taken to Poland but would be released in the following days. The 42nd Motorised Rifle Regiment, which entered Czechoslovakia at 0200 hours, reached Česká Skalice at 0530 hours. By 1000 hours, the units were at Hradec Kralove, where they tried to avoid conflict with the city's population. Yak-28R reconnaissance aircraft flew over the city's air base at 0500 hours, followed by fully armed Yak-27s or Yak-28Ps. The first Soviet aircraft then landed at Hradec Kralove, followed by about 50 MiG-17As from the 42nd Guards Fighter Bomber Aviation Regiment.[48]

At 1400 hours, General Siwicki, faced by the slowing down of his troops, ordered that all their objectives be reached by the evening. He also prohibited the requisitioning of equipment from the Czechoslovak authorities; all the needs of the Polish forces had to come from Poland. Siwicki ordered his men to strengthen the protection of ground they held, to establish continuous liaison with the 2nd Army forward command post located 4km northeast of Hradec Kralove and to monitor public order in the cities.

The Polish 10th Tank Division, which was to take control of eastern Bohemia, left its departure bases around Pietrowice and Plisz to engage along two axes, the first following the road from Lanškroun to Chrudim and the second that through Plisz to Havlíčkův Brod. On the first route, they went through Šumperk and Ústí nad Orlicí; on the second, they passed Bystřice nad Pernštejnem, Žďár nad Sázavou and Golčův Jeníkov.[49]

Polish troops on the streets of Olomuc on the morning of 21 August 1968. Even if hopeless, the resistance by the local population delayed the advance of the 10th Tank Division by nearly 12 hours.

A T-54/55, probably from the Polish 10th Tank Division, trundling down the main street of a town in northern Czechoslovakia. Notable is the application of not only the Polish national insignia and the turret number, but also of neat white identification strips down the glacis and the turret side.

On the first axis, Polish paratroopers attacked the SNB headquarters in Krnov at 0015 hours, where they disarmed the security corps agents. In Opava, where the 5th Tank Base of the ČSLA was located, Polish soldiers of the 13th Tank Regiment faced off against armed Czechoslovak soldiers, but there were no clashes. At 0200 hours, the Poles reached Rymerov, then advanced to Sobotin and finally Šumperk, where they found their passage blocked by civilian demonstrators. Due to the subsequent delay of several hours, the division's commander, Brigadier General Koper, ordered other units to avoid using the main roads and instead to take side roads.[50]

The Polish 17th Motorised Rifle Regiment was responsible for occupying northern Moravia in the region of Rokytnice v Orlických horách and Ústí nad Orlicí. At 0400 hours, the regiment set out on the Bystryca Klodzka axis at Žamberk. At the end of the day, its 1st Battalion was 2km west of Žamberk, the 2nd Battalion 2km west of Rychnov nad Kneznou and the 3rd Battalion east of Usti nad Orlici. The 25th Motorised Rifle Regiment reached Moravský Beroun at 0200 hours and Šternberk at 0530 hours, moving on to Olomouc, where it faced protests by the local population. These demonstrations also succeeded in halting the progress of the 2nd Tank Regiment, which followed the vanguard. But it was the units of the 10th Tank Division that were most affected by the protesting population, and they did not reach their targets until the night of 21/22 August. Despite these difficulties, a total of 12,846 Polish soldiers, 456 tanks, 320 APCs, 178 guns and 2,564 other military vehicles were on Czechoslovakian soil by the evening of 21 August.[51]

The Soviet 24th Motorised Rifle Division (181st Tank Regiment and 7th, 274th and 310th Motorised Rifle Regiments) was charged with occupying the rest of Moravia. It entered Czechoslovak territory between Hlučín and Český Těšín, and went southwest to Olomouc and Vsetín, which it reached in four hours after a journey of about 120km. Early in the morning, the 181st Tank Regiment occupied Mosnov air base southwest of Ostrava, where the ČSLA 8th Fighter Regiment was located. Shortly before 0400 hours, Soviet Su-7B/BM/U fighters of the 1st Guards Fighter-Bomber Aviation Regiment from Kunmadaras in Hungary landed there, along with up to 10 Yak-28Rs.[52]

The Invasion of Slovakia

The 38th Army's goal was to occupy most of Slovakia. The 31st Tank Division (77th Guards Tank Regiment, 100th and 237th Tank Regiments and 322nd Motorised Rifle Regiment) and the 15th Tank Division (29th, 239th and 244th Guards Tank Regiments and 295th Guards Motorised Rifle Regiment) advanced along the axis from Vyšné Německé to Žilina. The 128th Motorised Rifle Division (398th Guards Tank Regiment, 315th and 327th Guards Motorised Rifle Regiments and 487th Motorised Rifle Regiment) and the 30th Guards Motorised Rifle Division (30th Guards Tank Regiment and 164th, 166th and 168th Guards Motorised Rifle Regiments) followed the road from Maovce to Banská Bystrica.[53]

The progress of these divisions was smooth, with the exception of two incidents. The first was near Poprad, around 0400 hours, in the column led by General Mayorov, commander of the 38th Army. As the column halted, a T-55 tank collided with the general's Volga car, killing the sergeant sat next to him. The security commander, Colonel Spirin, wanted to imprison the tankers responsible, but Mayorov preferred to continue the journey to Trenčín.[54] The second incident took place at Košice around 0200 hours, when some of 128th Motorised Rifle Division's APCs opened fire on a crowd trying to prevent them from

A column of OT-64 APCs of the Polish army waiting for a signal to move early on 21 August 1968. The use of main roads by invading forces quickly proved a bad idea, as many of these were blocked by civilian demonstrators. Following hours of delays, the forces involved in Operation Danube thus began moving along secondary roads – though this change of tactics required an order from above.

Smoke billowing from the scene off the bloody confrontation between the troops of the Soviet 128th Motorised Rifle Division and local civilians in Košice, early on 21 August 1968, during which seven Czechoslovaks were killed by invaders.

moving forward. Seven civilians were killed. Mayorov then ordered the commanders of all his divisions to accelerate their progress.[55]

Around noon, the Soviets reached Trenčín, the Eastern Military District HQ. They were not made welcome, General Kodaje of the ČSLA informed them that he viewed them as occupiers. Mayorov arrived at about 1400 hours with his forward command post, surrounded by 10 tanks. When he entered the HQ building, no one answered his salute. He then explained the situation and Kodaje agreed to lend him some offices. Finally, the command post was set up on the banks of the Váh River, at the same place as it had during the Šumava exercise.[56]

The Bulgarian 12th Motorised Rifle Division participated in Operation Danube as part of 38th Army. It left Žnatina in Ukraine at 0200 hours, crossed the border in the region of Velké Kapušany and travelled 120km to the town of Košice, where the Bulgarians were halted by barricades of cars and trams. A group of young men threw stones, bricks and other objects at them, breaking the windows of between 40 and 50 vehicles and damaging five radio antennae. The Bulgarian column only passed through the city with difficulty. It was then forced to stop again at Rožňava, where, despite calls from the local KSČ, a crowd occupied the road and refused to move for an hour. Here, the column faced its first armed attack, since one of the vehicles was hit by three bullets. A Soviet tank company and several APCs, which formed the rear of the column, had to open fire to secure both sides of the road and allow the Bulgarians to cross the city. They finally entered Zvolen the next morning.[57]

The Hungarian 8th Motorised Rifle Division was also subordinated to the 38th Army. It entered southern Slovakia along three routes. The first axis, followed by the 14th Motorised Rifle Regiment, was along the Balassagyarmat road to Nové Mesto nad Váhom. The second axis – taken by the 31st Tank Regiment, 22nd Artillery Regiment, 93rd Anti-tank Artillery Section, 33rd Motorised Rifle Regiment and the division headquarters – went from Šahy to Sered. The third route followed the road from Letkés to Nové Zámky and was taken by the 63rd Motorised Rifle Regiment. Hungarian troops enjoyed the protection of around 100 fighter-jets and up to 10 helicopters.

Along the Hungarians' first axis, the 14th Motorised Rifle Regiment initially met little by way of obstacles, but little by little, the situation changed radically. In Nové Mesto nad Vohom, it faced a crowd of 700–800 people who began threatening them. The Hungarian commander therefore sent 10 tanks to encircle the city's officer school and called on their leaders to cooperate. While the Czechoslovak military accepted the demand, the demonstrations by civilians continued.[58]

On the second axis of the Hungarian 8th Motorised Rifle Division, the 31st Tank Regiment experienced a drama during the morning when a tank, after crossing a bridge over the Ipe River, skidded on the bank and fell down a slope, causing the death of a tanker. At Šahy station, two SNB policemen approached a BTR-50P APC and tried to explain to the Hungarians that they were lost because they were in Czechoslovak territory. One of the officers was immediately disarmed, but his colleague managed to escape. The Hungarian forces then took care to cut communications at post offices and railway stations so that no report of the invasion could be sent further inside the country. The Hungarians arrived at Levice at 0420 hours, where they blockaded the barracks of the 64th Tank Regiment of the ČSLA and occupied the administrative buildings of the city, the post office and the railway station.

From Levice, where most of the 31st Armoured Regiment remained, the Hungarian column was divided into three groups: the first and third groups, with the 22nd Artillery Regiment and 93rd Anti-tank Artillery Regiment, continued to advance towards Nitra and Hlohovec, while the second group headed southwest towards Sered. A reconnaissance group was the first to enter Nitra, where it met groups of civilians who demonstrated their hostility by throwing stones. Consequently, Hungarian soldiers took the city's representatives to the outskirts, where they had a brief meeting with the commander of the 8th Motorised Rifle Division, Major General Béla Lakatos. The Czechoslovaks said that they would not resist but would oppose the occupation and reject any agreement. The situation in the city, where crowds of demonstrators in the main square were increasingly

To safeguard their mobility, all Soviet and allied units participating in Operation Danube brought their full complement of bridging equipment, including GSP-55 self-propelled amphibious ferries, two of which are visible in the foreground of this photograph, together with a T-54 main battle tank.

A T-54/55 of the 63rd Motorised Rifle Regiment crossing the Ipe River on a pair of deployed GSP-55 ferry units.

aggressive, led the commander of the Hungarian regiment to shoot into the air, which caused the crowds to disperse without any injuries. However, around noon, a MiG-15 passing over the city announced that a crowd of 200–250 people had gathered again. A flight of four MiG-21s finally managed to disperse them. Around 1300 hours, the Hungarians in the third group then arrived at Hlohovec, and those of the second group in Sereď, occupying both cities without difficulty.[59]

Along the third axis of advance, the 63rd Motorised Rifle Regiment arrived in Štúrovo to neutralise the SNB District building. They drove up to the entry to the building's courtyard, taking aim with their guns and small arms, threatening to throw grenades inside if the occupants did not surrender. The Czechoslovak police were obliged to obey. The barracks of the ČSLA were surrounded at 0200 hours by about 300 soldiers with 120mm mortars, and then stormed. The ČSLA troops were awoken and kept under threat of arms before being driven out of the barracks.

The 3rd Company of the 63rd Motorised Rifle Regiment went directly to Nové Zámky but encountered difficulties between Letkés and Salka where the bridge over the Ipe River proved too fragile. The company had to install a pontoon bridge, which delayed its progress. It did not arrive at Nové Zámky until 0330 hours, when the designated battlegroups immediately began occupying important buildings and blocking access to the city. At 0500 hours, the regimental commander summoned the city leaders, but the situation began to deteriorate and a mass demonstration broke out in the main square around noon. The Hungarian unit there fired several times into the air, after which the company commander decided it was best to withdraw to avoid bloodshed, ordered the main forces to pull back outside the city.[60]

On the evening of 21 August, the 38th Army dominated the whole region. The 24th Motorised Rifle Division was southwest of Ostrava, the 128th Motorised Rifle Division south of Olomouc, the 254th Motorised Rifle Division southwest of Brno, the 48th Motorised Rifle Division northeast of Nova Mita and the 30th Guards Motorised Rifle Division south of Zvolen. The invasion of southern Slovakia, including Bratislava, was entrusted to the Southern Front from Hungary.

For the Southern Group of Forces, the main difficulty was the crossing of the Danube. The Soviet 13th Motorised Rifle Division was to cross the river at Komárno and the 254th Motorised Rifle Division at Medveďov and Bratislava. The 48th and 254th Motorised Rifle Divisions were to take control of southwestern Slovakia and part of Moravia, including the cities of Brno and Bratislava. The 13th Motorised Rifle Division progressed on the Komárno axis to Ceske Budejovice via Bratislava, with its right flank advancing towards Brno, Jihlava, Tábor and Písek and the left flank towards Český Krumlov, Prachatice and Vimperk. The 48th Motorised Rifle Division headed directly to Brno, the second largest city in Czechoslovakia.[61]

Despite local resistance by civilians, in general, Operation Danube proceeded as planned and the WTO forces secured most of Czechoslovakia during the early hours of 21 August 1968. By the evening, Soviet armoured vehicles – like this BTR-152 mounting a ZPU-2 anti-aircraft machine gun – were deployed in front of every major building in the country.

Around 2300 hours on 20 August, the armoured and motorised columns passed through Komárno. The first vehicles arrived in Bratislava around 0100 hours on the 21st, but it was only around 0800 hours that the Soviets occupied the city, disarming the ČSLA units and setting up their headquarters in Bratislava Castle. Around the Slovak capital, residents took to the streets, built barricades, threw stones at the tanks and encircled the Soviet consulate.[62]

Around 1000 hours, the Soviets arrived at Senica nad Myjavou, while the 13th Guards Tank Division reached Mikulov around 0800 hours and headed for Brno. The occupation of this city followed a similar pattern to that of Prague. On the evening of 20 August, at 2100 hours, a civilian AN-24 landed at Brno–Tuřany airport, carrying 20 passengers wearing Aeroflot uniforms.[63] It was only around 0100 hours that they lit up the take-off and landing zone, while the AN-12 started its engines to generate the electric current for the guidance device. Several other military AN-12s from the 3rd Military-Transport Aviation Division then landed, carrying the 350th Regiment of the 103rd Guards Airborne Division. In less than 10 minutes, the Soviets took control of the airport, ensuring the safe landing of the main force with the help of a group led by the commander of the ČSLA 10th Air Army, General Kúkel. From 0330 hours, 75 AN-12s landed paratroopers, ASU-57 and ASU-85 self-propelled guns and SPG-9 anti-tank guns, with the force then going on to Brno.[64] A similar airborne operation took control of the Náměšť nad Oslavou military air base.[65]

At 0700 hours, Soviet paratroopers blocked all roads, bridges, and exits from Brno. They invested the railway station, the main post office, the central telegraph building, the administrative buildings, the printing works and the radio and television stations, as well as the military installations of the ČSLA, Špilberk Castle and the buildings of the KSČ. By dawn, inhabitants had already gathered in the streets and squares and the bravest among them threw sticks and stones at the Soviet soldiers, while others tried to overturn cars. To repel the crowd, the Soviets retaliated by firing shots, killing two civilians and seriously injuring four others.[66] At noon, the first units of the 27th Guards Tank Regiment of the 13th Guards Tank Division arrived on the southern outskirts of Brno, linking up with the paratroopers. An hour later, the 103rd Guards Airborne Division was subordinated to the Southern Front.[67] The 13th Guards Tank Division continued its progress, reaching Ceske Budejovice and then Sušice at 1530 hours.[68]

Within a few hours, WTO forces had taken control of all Czechoslovak territory, occupying political and military centres, communication hubs and major military areas by the early hours of 21 August. To carry out these tasks, they received Czech support, mainly from local StB, SNB and KSČ groups. Their role was important, because the operation took place largely at night and, in many places, road signs were removed or reversed. For its part, the ČSLA did not resist. In several cases, WTO forces attempted to disarm Czechoslovak units, but for the most part they merely blockaded their vehicles, prohibited travel and ensured that weapons and ammunition remained in the ČSLA depots.[69] Czechoslovakia was subject to an air blockade with MiG-21PF/PFMs from bases in the GDR, Poland and Hungary, but also Yak-27R/28Rs and Il-28Rs.[70]

The 16th Air Army assigned a large number of units to Operation Danube. Fighter-jets from the 16th Division provided air protection for Central Front troops and occupied a number of airports in northern and western Bohemia. The reconnaissance activities were carried out by Il-28R and Yak-27R/28R aircraft. During the first days of Operation Danube, squadrons of the 16th Air Army were transferred to airports in southern, western and northern Bohemia. From Hungary, the 36th Air Army conducted reconnaissance operations and occupied airports in southern Bohemia and Slovakia. For this it mobilised 111 fighters, 31 fighter-bombers, 30 bombers and 23 reconnaissance aircraft. The 14th Air Army, whose 131st Fighter Aviation Division was transferred to air bases in Poland, provided coverage for airborne units. The Polish Air Force mobilised 13 Lim-2R reconnaissance aircraft and about 30 Mi-8T, Mi-2 and Mi-4 helicopters that covered the 2nd Army but also participated in the operations of the 1st Assault Battalion against radio transmitters. The Hungarian Air Force contributed 55 MiG-21s, 44 MiG-15s, up to 10 Mi-1 helicopters and a Li-2 transport aircraft to Operation Danube.[71]

Although Operation Danube was a success, it had nevertheless experienced some problems. Technical failures had often slowed progress along the roads. Some units were lost and became mixed with others. With so many soldiers and items of military equipment deployed, this was quite understandable, and the Soviets had given proof of their great operational mastery. They perfectly organised the simultaneous progress of nearly 30 divisions, a quarter of which were not Soviet, to neutralise and control the whole of Czechoslovakia. In addition, the operation was supposed to be an action carried out without the use of weapons. Success was thus based on the presence of sufficient forces to intimidate the Czechoslovaks.

The success of the operation was mainly the work of Grechko and Pavlovsky. Settled in Legnica, Pavlovsky received constant calls from Grechko to ask him where the divisions were, where the roadblocks were and to order him not to leave his command post without his consent. A few hours later however, Grechko blamed him for not going immediately to Prague: Pavlovsky and his staff went to Ruzyně, where they landed around 0500 hours in an empty and calm airport. Lieutenant General Yamschikov was waiting for him to see General Dzúr of the ČSLA Staff.[72] At the same time, Kirill Trofimovich Mazurov,[73] a member of the CPSU Politburo and Vice-President of the Council of Ministers of the USSR, arrived by air, sent by Brezhnev to supervise the Soviet forces in Czechoslovakia. He appeared officially in a colonel's uniform under the name of General Trofimov.[74]

7
NORMALISATION

Operation Danube was an indisputable military success, but its political component was a disaster. Officially, Dubček was still at the head of the KSČ and the invasion of the country had welded behind him the vast majority of the population including those who could be hostile to him. The Kremlin thus found itself in a dead end and searching for ways to resolve a crisis that the operation had only amplified.

Czechoslovak civil resistance

The first information about the invasion began to spread among the Czechoslovak population shortly after midnight. In Prague, this caused a general upheaval, with people gathering in the streets of the city from 0300 hours, and this phenomenon also occurred nearly everywhere else. They brandished Czechoslovak flags, along with portraits of Svoboda and Dubček. While the WTO forces had not met resistance from the ČSLA, they now had to face of civilians who, with the help of almost all the media in the country, organised a non-violent national resistance.

Although the operation of the national radio station was stopped shortly after the declaration of the KSČ Presidium was announced by order of Hoffmann, it resumed broadcasting normally during the morning. Dubček's opponents had forgotten that the National Radio had 16 auxiliary studios in and around Prague that continued to broadcast.[1] It was at this point that the first protesters began to gather in front of the radio building, and a large group of police and StB agents arrived to block the entrance to the protesters and employees.

At the same time, StB men tried to stop the programmes being broadcast, but without success. The radio continued to broadcast until the arrival of Soviet troops around 0800 hours. Radio distributed the Presidium statement to the Czechoslovak people and informed them of the progress of the invasion. During subsequent broadcasts, different resolutions were aired in the country and around the world to defend the reform process and condemn the armed intervention. In Brno, after the occupation of the radio station, it started transmitting again from the transmitter at Kojal, 25km from the city, with programmes relayed by the Austrian ORF television station.[2] In these circumstances, radio became not only a source of information, but also the coordinator and organiser of passive resistance. For example, on 22 August, the underground radio station Pilsen reported: "Do not provide the occupying forces with any information, any products, [nor] make any contact with them."[3]

Shortly before 0700 hours, Czechoslovak television also began broadcasting in Prague. Since the Petřín transmitter was occupied by WTO troops, the Cukrák transmitter at Strakonice – at an altitude of 411 metres – ws used instead.[4] Oldrich Sebor, who headed the 7th StB department that controlled communications, refused to cut off radio and television transmissions. On 22 August, he even stopped the jamming of Radio Free Europe broadcasts.[5] Special editions of the main Czechoslovak daily papers also published the resolution of the KSČ Presidium, while *Rudé Právo*'s editorial included its own proclamation of support for Dubček.[6]

The media's condemnation of the invasion of the country expressed the unequivocal rejection of the return to neo-Stalinism imposed by force. The situation reminded many Czechoslovaks of the fate of their country as a result of the Munich Agreement in 1938. This trauma, which still lived in the collective consciousness, was reactivated in the early hours of 21 August. It found expression on the walls of cities with the slogans 'Munich 1938 – Moscow 1968', 'Warsaw Munich!' and '1939 Hácha, Moravec[7] – 1968 Indra, Biľak, Kolder !'.[8] Civilians also ran between tanks and armoured vehicles to paint white swastikas and other Nazi symbols on the vehicles. Graffiti painted on walls – including the famous 'Lenin, come back, Brezhnev went crazy!' – pavements and sometimes even

With the nation's political leadership taken out of action during the early hours of 21 August, Czechoslovaks were left with few options but passive resistance. This truck collected graffiti, some comparing the USSR's invasion of 1968 with that of Hitler in 1938-1939.

tanks expressed the refusal to accept the occupation. Many Czechoslovak soldiers took part in these demonstrations, while officers threw away their Soviet medals.[9]

Despite requests from the authorities, acts of violence against the invaders were committed. There were many reports of civilians attacking the WTO military with stones and sticks. In some cases, armed attacks were launched, while monuments in memory of the Soviet liberators of 1945 were destroyed in towns and villages. According to General Mayorov, up until 23 August, seven APCs of the 38th Army were burned with incendiary bottles, and more than 300 vehicles were destroyed or damaged.[10]

One of the expressions of civil resistance to the occupation was the anonymising of cities. Signs indicating the names of localities and municipalities, offices and streets were obscured so they could not be seen or were rotated to point in a different direction. This form of resistance was intended to complicate or, if possible, prevent the orientation of the occupants in an unknown environment, and was initially very effective. Barricades, strikes, demonstrations and a refusal to cooperate were also part of the struggle against the WTO troops.

This trailer used as a barricade received similar graffiti, comparing 'Soviet Communist methods' with those of the Fascists in the late 1930s.

The third kind of inscription widespread in Czechoslovakia in the summer of 1968 was more direct, demanding that the 'Soviet aggressors go home'.

At the beginning of the occupation, the crowds of civilians spreading through the streets sought to persuade WTO soldiers by words and argument that there was no counter-revolution in the country.[11] A French archaeologist who was present later said:

> I crossed villages, there were tanks everywhere […] and all the people who were talking and who, not insulting, but shouting if I dare to say [at] the tankers. It was not an atmosphere of terror. These were obviously extremely stormy debates. I once heard Russian soldiers say: 'But we are coming to deliver you, we have been told that there are 40,000 American and West German soldiers disguised as tourists.' They were very surprised to be so badly received when they thought they were coming to liberate.[12]

However, the population quickly realised that speeches and dialogue with the occupying forces could give the impression that the invaders were welcome in the country. Consequently, the persuasive attitude gave way to passive resistance and the occupants were ignored, with the squares and public spaces abandoned by the crowds.[13]

The occupation forces tried to break this civil resistance by creating the 'Vltava' radio station, operating from Dresden, which broadcast information justifying "international aid" from the WTO countries, while newspapers in Berlin, Sofia, Warsaw, Budapest and Moscow claimed this was a new station broadcasting from Czechoslovak territory. The Soviet Army also distributed leaflets that were launched from helicopters and featured information from the Soviet TASS news agency.[14] It also tried to silence any media that opposed the invasion. On 22 August, paratroopers from the 103rd Division seized nine radio stations broadcasting 'counter-revolutionary' programmes. The following day in Prague, at 0300 hours, a unit of the 7th Airborne Division stopped the distribution of newspapers and leaflets and seized equipment from a clandestine printing press. On 24 August, they formed mobile groups to hunt underground radio stations and distributors of newspapers and leaflets.

On 23 August, in Brno, Soviet paratroopers prevented a massive demonstration from taking place. At 1400 hours, a strike began in the city to protest against the presence of Soviet troops. All traffic was stopped. To deal with the situation, 20 reconnaissance patrol vehicles were deployed from Vitebsk airfield to reinforce the 103rd Guards Airborne Division. Civil resistance continued during the following days. On the 25th, demonstrations took place in some parts of Prague. Many officers of the Czechoslovak Staff and Defence Ministry were openly hostile to the WTO military. Staff at Ruzyně airport refused to deal with Soviet aircraft.[15] Shootings occasionally broke out at night in the streets of Prague, but the days remained calm. On the 26th, in Brno, a short strike took place; around 1230 hours, people began to gather in the town square. Soviet paratroopers prevented the construction of barricades.[16]

In the first days of the invasion, the population's unequivocal refusal to accept the occupation was almost total and expressed itself openly.

Strengthening the military occupation

On 21 and 22 August, there were 20 divisions of the Warsaw Pact in Czechoslovakia. Over the next two days 10 more divisions entered the country – while 85–100 further divisions were stationed in the European part of the USSR, with an additional 70–80 divisions in Poland, the GDR, Hungary and Bulgaria.[17] By 25 August, 12 tank divisions, 13 motorised rifle divisions, two airborne divisions, and a powerful air force – totalling some 6,300 tanks, 2,000 guns, 550 fighter-jets and 250 transport aircraft – occupied Czechoslovakia.[18] The arrival of these new troops demonstrated the discomfort and fears of the Soviet Staff. They had thought that the majority of Czechoslovaks would be either favourable or passive to them; it had no expectation of such passive, spontaneous and above all large-scale resistance.

From 22–23 August, the Soviets occupied cities where they were previously absent, including Příbram, Tábor and Benešov in central Bohemia. The 1st Guards Motorised Rifle Division, which was in reserve in the GDR, was moved to the Kladno area. On 26 August, the Soviets asked the Poles to transport the Soviet 28th Army to Czechoslovakia. They also asked the NVA 11th Motorised Rifle Division to be ready in the region of Oelsnitz-Erbestock-Adorf-Plauen, but the order to cross the border did not come and the division was stood down on 31 August.[19]

For its part, the Polish Army regrouped and completed the movement of its forces, including the 10th and 11th Tank Divisions, while on 23 August, the 25th Motorised Rifle Division moved to Šumperk. On that day, the command of the 2nd Army moved to Hradec Airport to review the situation. Major General Tadeusz Tuczapski and Brigadier General Wojciech Barański believed that the Polish forces were too weak in the vast territory that they occupied. The Defence Minister, General Jaruzelski, therefore transferred, under Siwicki's authority, the 4th Motorised Rifle Division, which was reinforced with the 27th Tank Regiment. These forces set up on 25 August around Milovice and Mlada Boleslav. The Polish CoS ordered the commander of the Warsaw Military District Division, General Zygmunt Huszc, to deploy the 6th Airborne Division in the Rychnov nad Kněžnou-Červená Voda area in eastern Bohemia. However, General Siwicki was still dissatisfied with the number of troops under his command and said he could not carry out his duties, including the monitoring of ČSLA units.[20]

The situation seemed no better in the area occupied by Hungarians, who noted their unpopularity among Slovaks and even Hungarians living in Slovakia. On 23 August, the commander of the 8th Motorised Rifle Division summoned ČSLA and SNB commanders, the secretaries of the KSS and the chiefs of the StB in the area under his control and ordered them to have inscriptions against the invasion erased and to stop the actions of the "agitators", under pain of arrest.[21]

The Hungarian Defence Minister, Czinege, quickly realised that in such situation, the forces of the 8th Division were not enough, so asked for help from the Soviets. They refused, saying this was a problem the Hungarians had to solve themselves. As the division did not have the capacity to ensure order, the Hungarian authorities brought in 300 personnel of the Interior Ministry armed with batons and four water cannons, which deployed from Levice. Transportation of food and other supplies from Hungary was carried out daily by a column of 30–70 vehicles, protected by a special group of the 6th Motorised Rifle Regiment. Persistent tensions prompted General Provalov to order the Hungarians not to divide their forces into smaller groups, and that unit commanders should move only in APCs or helicopters, and always with the same security detail. Ordinary soldiers were not allowed to move without weapons or ammunition.[22]

While the Bulgarian 22nd Motorised Rifle Regiment was guarding Ruzyně and Vodochody Airports, the 12th Motorised Rifle Regiment, after a night spent in front of Zvolen, entered the city at 0500 hours on 22 August, blockading the ČSLA barracks. It also occupied Sliač air base, located nearby, where conflict broke out with Czechoslovak soldiers. At 0800 hours, the rest of the regiment occupied Banská Bystrica in central Slovakia, where it took control of the printing works and the local newspaper, radio station, post office, telegraph and the KSS and SNB buildings.[23]

Military aviation was particularly active in the days following the invasion. Up until 5 September, 25 AN-12s of the 708th Military Transport Aviation Regiment carried 772 paratroopers, 19 military vehicles and 60 tons of cargo to Brno Airport. The AN-12Bs of the 334th Military Transport Aviation Regiment had made 185 take-offs by 25 August and carried a total of 1,522 troops and 137 tons of cargo between Vitebsk and Brno and between Chkalovsky and Prague.[24] In total, the 12th Military Transport Aviation Division made 393 flights during Operation Danube, carrying 3,930 people and 1,130 tons of cargo. The 3rd, 6th and 18th Guards Military Transport Aviation Divisions also participated in the operation. As of 21 August,

Despite the deployment of about 20 divisions inside Czechoslovakia by the evening of 21 August, the commanders of the WTO forces still felt in a weak position and even 'threatened'. Unsurprisingly, during the first days after the invasion, their forces frequently bivouacked like these Soviet airborne troops, in circular camps, providing all-round defence.

fighter-jets and bombers were deployed in Czechoslovakia, but their number continued to grow, especially on 25 and 26 August, when General Alexander Pokryskin at the Military Council of the 8th Air Defence Army ordered 28 Yak-28Ps to be sent to Ostrava-Mosnov Airport, 36 MiG-19Ps to České Budějovice–Ianá Air Base and 36 MiG-19Ps to Žatec Air Base.[25]

The determination of the Czechoslovak people to defend their liberties and support the reforming leadership made the occupying forces strengthen their presence in order to carry out policing missions for which they were not prepared. There was a great risk that an incident would degenerate into bloodshed, which would lead to Moscow losing control of the situation and provoke an international crisis. Without a political solution to the crisis opened by the invasion, the Kremlin found itself in a stalemate, left only with the choice of establishing a strict occupation regime or searching for a political compromise based on a just evaluation of the balance of power in Czechoslovakia. The uncompromising civil resistance of the Czechoslovakian people proved an effective weapon against Moscow, forcing the Soviets to abandon their original plan and to improvise.[26]

Three Soviet An-12s and a Lisunov Li-2 seen at a Czechoslovak airport in mid-August 1968. By then, these aircraft had flown more than 300 sorties in support of Operation Danube.

Vehicles of the Polish mechanised forces – including an OT-64 APC – at an occupied Czechoslovak air base.

Negotiations in Moscow

On the evening of 21 August, the Soviet ambassador in Washington, Dobrynin, requested a hearing with the US President to deliver a statement to him saying that because of the deterioration of the situation in Czechoslovakia, the "result of an internal conspiracy outside" which attacked the existing social order, "the Prague government asked the allied states, including the Soviet Union, to provide direct assistance, including the participation of military forces".[27] The surprised Americans immediately convened their National Security Council and adopted a cautious solution, rejecting the use of armed force and publishing a statement of disapproval, but called for the convening of the United Nations Security Council. The same day, Secretary of State Dean Rusk spoke to Dobrynin and announced the position of the US government, which involved issuing an official statement saying Rusk and Dobrynin had met for a consultation on the situation in Czechoslovakia. However, informally, he told the Soviet ambassador that the United States did not understand why the Soviet version of a "request of the Government of the Czechoslovak Socialist Republic" did not agree with the statement broadcast on Czech radio and why Moscow had claimed that external forces "attacked Czechoslovakia".[28]

The next day, in response to the negative reaction of international opinion to the invasion, President Johnson issued a clearer but still very moderate position: "The reasons given by the Soviet Union seem inaccurate. The Czechoslovak government has not asked its allies

Like other occupying troops, Polish forces found themselves exposed to passive means of resistance – primarily in the form of slogans applied on every suitable building, and usually comparing the 'Soviet' invasion of 1968 with that of Nazi Germany of 1938.

to interfere in its internal affairs. No external aggression threatened Czechoslovakia."[29] Washington's rejection of the argument that would provide a legal basis for the invasion worried Moscow, especially since the majority of Communists in Prague continued to support Dubček.

Politically beaten, the conservatives Biľak, Indra and Kolder were reprimanded by Brezhnev, who reproached them for their failed coup. All the constitutional institutions and the KSČ categorically opposed the invasion. The KSČ Prague Committee, which had expressed its agreement with the proclamation of the KSČ Presidium, attempted to convene a meeting of delegates to the 14th KSČ Congress for that afternoon. Several dozen members of the Central Committee also met to try to contact Dubček. They issued a resolution against the intervention, which was also signed by those who initially opposed the reform process. On their side, the government and the National Assembly unequivocally agreed to the proclamation of the KSČ Presidium. Through the media, they informed the public – and also Moscow – that they unequivocally condemned an invasion they considered "illegal" under international law and the principles of socialist internationalism.[30]

Buoyed by the military success of Operation Danube, Brezhnev called on the conservatives to set up a Peasant and Worker Government guaranteeing the political legitimacy of the invasion. He telephoned Svoboda to tell him the reasons for the occupation of Czechoslovakia. He also assured him that the WTO troops would not be occupiers; they would protect the sovereignty of the country and, when the "healthy forces" of the KSČ were in power, they would leave.[31]

Around 1000 hours on 21 August, Biľak, Indra and Kolder arrived at Prague Castle. The purpose of their visit was to persuade Svoboda to create the government wanted by Moscow. Their negotiations proved in vain, as Svoboda merely instructed the conservatives to write down their proposals and present them the following day.[32] Shortly after their departure, the president received a government delegation led by Minister Božena Machačová, who informed Svoboda of their willingness to continue his policy and asked for his support. The president was hesitant and spoke as if Černík and Dubček had resigned. He replied, however, that he accepted the government, under the chairmanship of Machačová, should continue its activities. During that evening, members of the KSČ Central Committee met delegates of the 14th Congress at the Hotel Praha. A group of conservatives was present. The meeting decided to convene the Congress delegates, but also voted on a compromise resolution that encouraged cooperation with the occupiers. However, this resolution was rejected by all the country's KSČ regional committees.[33]

The decision to hold the 14th KSČ Congress – initially scheduled for September – early was maintained. Delegates and organisers of the Congress began to meet in the Vysočany district of Prague, in the Elektrotechnika factory restaurant, in the early hours of 22 August. Shortly after 1000 hours, the meeting began with nearly 1,000 delegates. During the day, this figure increased to 1,543, but only five delegates came from Slovakia: not only were they hampered by the distance they would have to travel, but some Slovak delegates were arrested by the occupying forces.[34] Those at the Congress also included ČSLA, government and National Assembly representatives, while security was provided by the People's Militia.

Due to the secrecy of the Congress, only the most important issues were discussed. Delegates fully supported Dubček's reform policy, confirming the decision to continue to implement the ideas of the Action Programme and pursue the policy of democratic socialism. The Congress also adopted a statement in which it opposed military intervention and called on WTO troops to leave the country. Before ending in the early hours of 23 August, it proceeded to the election of a new Central Committee, which included Dubček.[35]

President Svoboda had been looking for a way to get his country out of its difficult situation by making concessions. He decided to go to Moscow to negotiate with Brezhnev, hoping to bring back the Presidium members interned in the USSR so that they could resign immediately after their return. Without the National Assembly's approval, he organised a delegation including Biľak, Piller and Indra,[36] ignoring the conclusions of the 14th KSČ Congress and showing he accepted Brezhnev's criticism of the reform process and its leaders. It was therefore not surprising that the Kremlin welcomed Svoboda's proposal: he offered a possible political solution to the crisis.

On 23 August, the Czechoslovak delegation – led by Svoboda, the conservatives Biľak, Indra and Piller, Justice Minister Kučera and Defence Minister Dzúr – boarded Soviet aircraft bound for Moscow. En route, they landed in Bratislava, where Deputy Prime Minister Gustav Husak joined them. Not long before, Dubček and Černík had been transferred to Moscow.[37] After his arrival, Dubček was taken to the Kremlin to meet Brezhnev, Kosygin and Podgorny, who explained to him what led to the invasion of his country, including the lask of respect for the undertakings of Čierna nad Tisou and Bratislava. Dubček tried to resist these arguments and refused to make any decision without the participation of other members of the Czechoslovak state.[38]

After the arrival of the Svoboda delegation, the opening discussions began. Brezhnev, Kosygin and Podgorny heard Indra explain why the conservatives' plan had failed. Only after these explanations did an interview with President Svoboda take place, first with Brezhnev, then with all the Soviet leaders. Around 1900 hours, discussions between the two groups began in earnest. Brezhnev opened the meeting by pointing out the mistakes of the Czechoslovakian reformist leadership and the threat of counter-revolution it posed to the country. Nevertheless, he accepted that Dubček, Černík and Smrkovský could be released and resume their responsibilities, but on condition that they fulfilled the obligations taken at Čierna nad Tisou and that the underground KSČ Congress be declared illegal.[39] He ended his speech with a threat, stating that it was not possible for the WTO troops to leave Czechoslovakia before finding a solution to the crisis.

After a speech by Kosygin supporting Brezhnev's position, Husak was the first to speak for the Czechoslovak delegation. He acknowledged that mistakes had been made but added that the Czechoslovak leadership had sufficient resources to solve them. Biľak, meanwhile, condemned the KSČ Congress as illegal and demanded

MiG-17F fighter-bombers of the Soviet air force at an occupied Czechoslovak air base.

its postponement. After this first meeting, Dubček and Černík arrived at the Kremlin that night, where they were able to meet the Czechoslovak delegation.[40]

On the morning of 24 August, as a meeting gathered around Brezhnev and the WTO leaders Zivkov, Kádár, Ulbricht and Gomułka, Smrkovský, Špaček, Šimon and Kriegel were transferred from Uzhhorod to Moscow. They were invited, with the exception of Kriegel, to meet Brezhnev, Podgorny and Kosygin, but they took the same stance as Dubček. Unable to break the solidarity of the KSČ leaders with Dubček, Podgorny, Ponomarev and Kosygin turned to Svoboda. The Soviets tried to persuade him to return to Czechoslovakia and sign an agreement. However, the President would not return without those whom he had promised to bring back. In the evening, a new discussion with the Czechoslovak representatives ended without agreement.[41]

On 25 August, Lenárt, Švestka, Jakes, Rigo, Barbírek and Mlynář arrived in Moscow. Shortly after, the KSČ Presidium held a meeting with Černík, but without Kriegel, Indra and Biľak. It was obvious to the Czechs that they had to compromise. It was a dramatic moment, with the KSČ officials under constant pressure. Their country was occupied by an army of half a million men, with the fear of possible bloodshed, the eventual establishment of a military occupation regime or the threat of a civil war. In addition, it was still possible that the reformers would not be allowed to return to Prague.

According to Černík's archives, he and Dubček, Svoboda and Smrkovský decided not to accept an agreement that would characterise the situation in Czechoslovakia as counter-revolutionary or would require the withdrawal of the 21 August Svoboda Declaration condemning the occupation. They also rejected a text that asserted that Czechoslovakia was threatened by NATO troops, that their policies threatened socialism in Central Europe and which called for the abolition of the Action Programme. Mlynář, Špaček and Šimon were responsible for drafting this agreement.[42]

A meeting of the representatives of the 'Warsaw Five' unambiguously rejected the Czechoslovak proposal and decided that they would be responsible for drafting the text of the agreement. As a result, the Soviet side submitted its protocol to the Czechoslovaks, who were split between those who wanted to sign the document and those who hesitated but Svoboda insisted that it be accepted.

Soviet MiG-21PF interceptors on the tarmac of an airport in the Prague area. Until Moscow was ready to trust the Czechoslovak armed forces again, they took over the task of defending the local airspace. Note the PT-76 light tank.

Operation Danube saw the first 'combat' deployment of the then newest MiG-21-variant: the MiG-21S, as shown in this photograph. This predecessor of the subsequent MiG-21M, MiG-21MF, and MiG-21bis variants, was the first version with four underwing pylons.

On 26 August, the final meeting between the Czechoslovak delegation and Soviet leaders in the Kremlin began at 1600 hours, the draft protocol having been distributed. Černík rejected the accusations against the reformers and expressed his willingness to resolve the situation by cancelling the 14th Congress and fulfilling the commitments of Čierná nad Tisou and Bratislava. At the same time, he called for the withdrawal of WTO troops from towns and villages.[43] Brezhnev then asked if any of those present had reservations about the text. Dubček responded by asking that the Czechoslovak proposal be included in the protocol. He then defended the reform process and condemned the WTO's intervention. Brezhnev, angry, spoke again. His speech was very critical of the reform process, and in particular Dubček. This was followed by criticism from Kosygin, who was even more vigorous. Finally, the Soviet Politburo left the room, only returning after a long break. The Czechoslovak delegation then agreed to sign the protocol.[44]

At 2245 hours, two documents were signed: the 'Communiqué on the Czechoslovak-Soviet Talks' and the 'Protocol on the Talks of the Delegation of the USSR and Czechoslovakia'.[45] The Protocol was a 15-point agreement in which the obligations of the Czechoslovak leaders were inscribed. Items 1 and 5 dealt with the stay and conditions of the WTO troops. Military matters were dealt with in points 6 and 9. On the political side, point 2 stated that the 14th KSČ Congress was null and void. In points 3 and 4, it was decided that it was necessary to normalise the situation in the country, to cooperate with the socialist countries and to consolidate the power of the KSČ in accordance with the Čierná nad Tisou agreements, i.e. to control the media and not to allow the existence of political clubs. Point 7 forced the Czechoslovak delegation not to retaliate against the "pro-Soviet forces", which on the contrary, according to point 12, were to benefit from the changes of personnel within the KSČ. Point 8 dealt with economic cooperation, while points 10 and 11 dealt with foreign policy, including the withdrawal of the Czechoslovakia question from the United Nations Security Council meeting. Point 13 provided for new negotiations, while the next item stated that the content of KSČ and CPSU leaders' meetings should remain secret.[46] The Moscow Protocol undeniably constituted a loss of sovereignty for Czechoslovakia, and although it remained secret, even for the majority of the KSČ Central Committee, it was felt by the population to be a diktat imposed by Moscow.

The Czechoslovak delegation could now return to their country. Brezhnev did not want to release Kriegel, who was the only one to refuse to sign the Moscow Agreement. Eventually, an aircraft to Prague for the whole Czechoslovak delegation was chartered on 26 August, landing the following morning. After his return, Dubček addressed the Czechoslovak people on 27 August. At the beginning of his speech, he thanked them for the trust they had placed in him and others. He stressed the need to consolidate and normalise the situation, which he feared would otherwise result in the restoration of order by measures limiting the degree of democracy and freedom of expression. The return of discipline, he said, had to allow the course of the reforms to continue. Despite the situation, Dubček's reformist leaders thus retained the sympathy and support of the Czechoslovakians.

The return from Moscow of the Czechoslovak delegation provoked joy among the population. At 1100 hours, the sirens of companies in Prague and Brno rang out to celebrate the event. In order to avoid conflict, the Soviet paratroopers of the 7th Guards Airborne Division withdrew from the headquarters of the government and the KSČ Central Committee building. On 30 August, in agreement with the Brno local authorities, the Soviets abandoned the television and radio buildings, the newsrooms of the regional newspaper and the transmitter station at Mount Gad 3km northeast of the city, having been assured that these media would not broadcast attacks against them.[47]

Gradually, the situation in the country returned to some sort of normality. In early September, walls and pavements were systematically cleaned of slogans, inscriptions and posters denouncing the intervention, beginning in Prague. In the capital and in other Czech cities, the Soviet Army abandoned the buildings it had occupied and withdrew to the outskirts. Only three airborne battalions remained in Prague, and just one in Brno.

At 1800 hours on 8 September, wreaths of flowers were laid in Prague on the monument to Soviet soldiers who died when the city was liberated in 1945, in the presence of representatives of Soviet troops, the Bulgarian Army, the KSČ and the Soviet Union and Czechoslovak states. A few days later, the soldiers guarding the Soviet embassy withdrew. By the end of 12 September, all units of the 7th and 103rd Guards Airborne Divisions had withdrawn from Prague and Brno.[48]

The Soviet Army installed in Czechoslovakia

The Moscow Protocol attached great importance to military matters and the deployment of Soviet troops in Czechoslovakia. This question began to be dealt with on 28 August with the establishment of a Czechoslovak Government Operational Group to organise the temporary stay of WTO troops in the country.[49] On 3 September, the Czechoslovak government revealed its position on the withdrawal of troops. It was to take place in three phases: the first would be the evacuation of the cities, then the troops were to withdraw along the western USSR border, and in the third phase they would evacuate the border with the FRG.[50] But the Soviets, who knew the occupation of the country remained their best means of applying pressure on the Czechoslovaks, were discreet about the issue of evacuation. During talks on 10 September and 3 and 4 October, they did not address this issue, and Marshal Ogarkov, who led the negotiations for the Soviets, even said that units would spend the winter in Czechoslovakia.[51]

Point 5 of the Moscow Protocol nevertheless provided for the conclusion of a treaty on the issue of the withdrawal of WTO troops and the deployment of Soviet troops, and the first such negotiations were held on 16 and 17 September in Mukachevo. The delegation was led by Defence Minister Dzúr and Marshal Grechko. For the Czechoslovaks, the withdrawal of WTO troops was a key issue to

The invasion and occupation of Czechoslovakia by the WTO forces continued facing – often fierce and certainly massive – public resistance for much of 1968, and well into 1969. The Soviet troops often felt especially vulnerable, for reasons obvious from this photograph of their T-54s, BTR-152s, and trucks in St. Wenceslas Square, in downtown Prague.

appease public opinion, which still saw them as occupation troops and with whom relations remained tense. Troops caused accidents, and soldiers harassed and assaulted civilians. On 7 September, a drunken Soviet soldier killed a 14-year-old apprentice in Prague, provoking anger among the population.[52] From 4 September to 18 October, 240 civilians were arrested, interrogated and sometimes beaten by soldiers, and 87 robberies were committed, 17 civilians were killed and eight women raped by WTO troops. Soviet vehicles also caused 160 road accidents.[53] These incidents were in addition to those that occurred during Operation Danube. The most dramatic event took place in front of the radio building in Prague, where 52 people were injured and 12 killed by an ammunition explosion, while three others were shot dead. In the early days of the occupation, dozens of people were injured. Overall, the occupation of Czechoslovakia resulted in 100 deaths, 335 serious injuries and hundreds of minor injuries. There were only about 20 deaths of WTO troops during the same period, of which just one, a Bulgarian soldier, was killed by Czechoslovak citizens.[54]

The Czechoslovak representatives apparently submitted a proposal based on the Soviet demands of previous years, namely the installation of one to two divisions in their territory. During a visit by Černík to Moscow on 10 September, Brezhnev and Kosygin had already proposed to suppress one to two Czechoslovakian divisions and some of the air force, which would be replaced by twice as many Soviet units. Kosygin even advanced the idea of leaving 250,000 Soviet soldiers in Czechoslovakia, an unrealistic figure since it was higher than the total number of ČSLA personnel.

Negotiations continued in Moscow during October. The treaty eventually signed on 16 October provided for the retention in Czechoslovakia of between 70,000 and 80,000 soldiers.[55] The Czechoslovak delegation was able to obtain only one major concession, namely the disappearance of Article 14 of the original treaty, which provided that, in the event of a threat to the security of Soviet troops in Czechoslovakia, the Soviet command could, with help from the ČSLA, take steps to eliminate this threat. The agreement was approved at a meeting of the National Assembly on 18 October and was signed by President Svoboda. The treaty also contained a secret protocol, which National Assembly members were not aware of. This set the number of soldiers at 75,000, with the transfer of depots, three hospitals, training areas and four air bases for 200 aircraft. Within two months, additional agreements had to be drawn up, regulating the specific aspects of the relations and lives of Soviet troops in Czechoslovakia.[56] The secret protocol also provided that Soviet air forces could fly over the territory of Czechoslovakia during combat training, as well as flights from Czechoslovakia to all neighbouring socialist countries.

From mid-October, 28 WTO divisions and 20 air regiments left Czechoslovak territory. The first contingents to withdraw were the Bulgarian, Hungarian, Polish and some of the Soviet divisions. By 8 November, about 86 percent of the soldiers had been withdrawn from Czechoslovakia. Operation Danube officially ended on 15 November 1968.[57]

The Soviet forces which, following the agreement of 16 October, remained in Czechoslovakia were organised in the Central Group of Forces (CGF), founded on 25 October, and placed under the command of General Mayorov. The CGF comprised the 15th Guards Tank Division, 30th Guards Motorised Rifle Division, 18th Guards Motorised Rifle Division, 31st Tank Division, 48th Motorised Rifle Division and 131st Mixed Aviation Division.[58]

Thanks to Operation Danube, the Soviet Command was able to achieve its fundamental strategic goal of bridging the gap between its groups of forces deployed in Central Europe. It could also, without violating the NPT, install nuclear weapons on Czechoslovak soil. Above all, the success of the operation ensured the respect of "international obligations towards the peace and socialism camp" by local political and military leaders.

Moscow had also improved its military position in relation to the FRG. Before August 1968, the ČSLA had 10 operational divisions and six other divisions that could be mobilised. After the deployment of the CGF, there were now 15 Soviet and Czechoslovak divisions, plus six Czechoslovak divisions that could be mobilised. In addition, all Soviet divisions at that time possessed tactical-level nuclear weapons.

The 'normalisation' of Czechoslovakia

Moscow's return of the Czechoslovak delegation signalled the beginning of the process called 'normalisation', which was based on the principles set out in the Moscow Protocol. Although the reformers were the first to take steps to establish this process – which caused disenchantment, resignation and apathy among the population – they were gradually removed from positions of power. Upon his return, Dubček's influence weakened, and he was replaced on 17 April 1969, at the direction of the KSČ, by Husák.[59] Dubček was sent as ambassador

The withdrawal of Polish mechanised troops from Czechoslovakia in late 1968. Notable are 'farewell' inscriptions on forward hulls of the OT-64s in this photograph, praising their return to the 'homeland'.

Another Polish OT-64 during the withdrawal from Czechoslovakia. Who exactly was expected to feel emboldened by inscriptions like 'Every Pole is a brave soldier', remains unclear.

A Soviet BRDM-1 amphibious scout car securing a crossroad in Bratislava in September 1968.

Soviet armoured vehicles – like this PT-76 amphibious tank and a BRDM-1 scout car – remained a frequent sight on the streets of all Czechoslovak urban centres until the official end of Operation Danube on 15 November 1968.

Irrespective of where in Czechoslovakia they deployed, vehicles of the occupation forces quickly found themselves 'decorated' with all sorts of graffiti or other 'insignia' – including Soviet flags overpainted with Swastikas, as in this case.

to Turkey and expelled from the KSČ. Prime Minister Černík resigned in January 1970, while Smrkovský was ousted as President of the National Assembly and lost his KSČ membership.[60] The leading personalities of the Prague Spring were now tightly controlled and monitored by the StB.

After securing control of the KSČ, Husak proceeded to eliminate the reformers from the party leadership, repeal the liberal measures of the Prague Spring, restore Party control over the economy, reinforce the position of state security agencies and return Czechoslovak foreign policy to a strict framework that was defined by the USSR.[61]

The reaffirmation of the KSČ's leading role was reflected in the ban on non-communist clubs and organisations such as Club 231 or KAN on 27 September. All media outlets whose editorial line did not agree with the new direction were closed. Half of the members of the Union of Czechoslovak Journalists were dismissed, while 45 of the 80 members of *Rudé Pravo*'s editorial board were dismissed for lack of loyalty. The government also established a Press and Information Office to 'guide' the topics covered by the press.[62]

The Writers' Union suffered a massive purge, with three-quarters of its members excluded from the organisation. Their books were removed from shops and libraries. Only 'ideologically verified' works that had passed censorship control were now authorised. Representatives of all sections of the Czechoslovak intelligentsia – not only writers and journalists – became the object of repression. A common form of punishment was dismissal, followed by the prohibition to practice a profession. Teachers, playwrights and historians then became taxi drivers, removal men or window cleaners. As a rule, children of victims could not access higher education, and sometimes even secondary education.

The StB, ČSLA and trade unions were also purged. In January 1970, at the initiative and under the direction of Husak, Biľak and Indra, a full verification of the reliability of KSČ members was carried out by special commissions. The test included an interview during which the militant had to show the 'correct' attitude towards the political line chosen by the party leaders. In 1970 and 1971, no fewer than 1,508,326 KSČ members were subjected to this procedure, of whom 326,817 (22 percent) were expelled from the Party. Even Kolder, one of the initiators of the entry of WTO troops into Czechoslovakia, was expelled from the KSČ leadership because of his support for Dubček in early 1968. In 1971, out of 115 members of the Central Committee, only 26 had been members before 1966.[63]

The normalisation process caused protests. On 16 January 1969, a student of Charles University, Jan Palach, committed suicide by self-immolation to protest against the nation's new political direction. Hundreds of thousands of people attended his funeral, which took place nine days later. On 25 February that year, another student, Jan Zajits, also set himself on fire on the 21st anniversary of the establishment of the communist regime, an example that Evžen Plocek followed two months later in Jihlava. On 28 March, after the victory of the Czechoslovak national team over the USSR at the World Ice Hockey Championships, thousands of people took to the streets of Prague to express their joy and attacked 21 Soviet barracks.[64] On 21 August 1969, on the first anniversary of the invasion, a mass demonstration took place in Prague. It was severely repressed by the police, supported by the 17th Tank Regiment, leading to the deaths of five people, while 33 more were injured.[65]

The ČSLA had been used to maintaining order in the country. Consequently, demonstrations were often repressed by force, such as those on 28 October 1969, or 7 and 8 November, when the police – reinforced by the People's Militia – used batons, water cannons and tear

A pair of Soviet Su-7BM fighter-bombers passing low above a Czechoslovak city in late August 1968.

A Soviet Army Zil-135 truck with BM-24 multiple rocket launcher (covered by a tarpaulin) withdrawing from Czechoslovakia in October 1968.

Normalisation had profoundly influenced Czechoslovak society, establishing a pure Leninist regime. Indeed, when Mikhail Gorbachev set up his policy of Glasnost and Perestroika from 1985 to renew the CPSU apparatus and the Soviet economy, the Czechoslovak State apparatus was incapable of any reform whatsoever. In 1977, dissidents founded the Charter 77 association, publicly reminding the government of its commitment to respect human rights signed in 1975 at the Helsinki Conference. In December 1976, a petition entitled 'Declaration of the Charter 77' began to circulate and to be signed by personalities from the world of the arts, university professors and ordinary citizens, which required the government to respect its commitments. However, the few hundred signatories were then imprisoned, and sometimes persecuted, by the regime.

The situation changed on 25 March 1988 with the so-called 'candlelight demonstration' in Bratislava, which became the first mass protest rally since the Prague Spring. Rapidly, demonstrations reached the capital: within 18 months, political demonstrations became a permanent part of city life. On 17 November 1989, a large student march was held in Prague. On the way to Wenceslas Square in the city centre, the police dispersed the crowd. One of the wounded students, fleeing the police, broke into a theatre building and announced the incident directly during the show. The following day, all theatres in Prague began an indefinite strike. On 20 November, the universities joined the strike. Thousands of demonstrations took place every day in Prague, led by the Civil Forum, a political movement created on 19 November by Charter 77 participants. Under popular pressure and unleashed by Moscow, the KSČ Presidium resigned on 24 November.

On 26 November, another large gathering took place in the centre of Prague, involving 750,000 people, or about 5 percent of the Czechoslovak population. Addressing the people, speakers from the Civil Forum and other organisations demanded the resignation of

gas against 6,000 demonstrators who built barricades in Prague.[66] A state of emergency was declared in some units of the ČSLA at the time of the self-immolation of Jan Palach and at his funeral, but also during the Czechoslovak ice hockey victory on 28 March 1969. The ČSLA thereby fully demonstrated its ability to fulfil "the internal functions of the army" and had the full confidence of political leaders when it was used to police the first anniversary of the invasion alongside the security forces. In 1969, its fighting abilities were restored and it regained its rank within the Warsaw Pact, as evidenced by its presence at the Shield 70 military exercise.[67]

Trucks of the Soviet Army re-crossing the border to Poland in September 1968.

Although highly successful as a military operation, in securing the deployment of the Soviet armed forces into the country, and facilitating the reinstallation of a Leninist regime in Prague, Operation Danube proved a political disaster with far-reaching consequences for all of the Warsaw Pact members. This photograph shows a Soviet mechanised column withdrawing from Czechoslovakia in October 1968.

the government. On the same day, demonstrations also took place in Bratislava, Brno and other cities.

Realising their inability to repress the protest by force, the communist government decided to make contact with the opposition. On 29 November, as a result of the negotiations between Vaclav Havel of the Civil Forum and Karel Urbanek, leader of the KSČ, the National Assembly annulled the article of the Czechoslovak Constitution on the leading role of the KSČ. On 10 December, the government and President Husak resigned. On 29 December, Parliament elected Dubček as its president and Vaclav Havel to the Czechoslovak presidency. At the same time, changes were taking place in the KSČ, which repudiated Stalinist ideology, recognised the principles of democracy and dismissed the People's Militia. Thus disappeared the communist regime in Czechoslovakia, a country embarking on the path of democratic reforms and the development of a market economy. At the end of 1992, the country was divided into two states – the Czech Republic and Slovakia – a decision disapproved of by Dubček, who died in November that year in a car accident.

On the Soviet side, in 1987, Gorbachev paid homage to Dubček and "socialism with a human face", before recognising in 1989 that the invasion of Czechoslovakia in 1968 was a mistake.[68] A few weeks after the fall of the Berlin Wall, the GDR People's Parliament apologised to the Czechoslovak people for the East German participation in Operation Danube. On 1 March 2006, in front of Czech President Vaclav Klaus, Russian President Vladimir Putin accepted for his country the moral but not the legal responsibility for the invasion.[69]

That same year, the Czech people demonstrated against the installation in the country of an American missile-radar defence.[70] This rejection of a foreign military presence shows that the trauma of the 1968 invasion – after that of 1938 – is still present in Czech society.

The invasion of Czechoslovakia in 1968 marked a turning point in the Cold War. On the Western side, while the *Détente* policy was not called into question, NATO had to adapt to the new strategic situation and the Soviet military build-up in Central Europe. The United States had therefore used this event to further involve its European allies in NATO structures that had been in crisis since the mid-1960s with the departure of France from the integrated command. Given the speed and scale of the invasion of Czechoslovakia, Western states, particularly the FRG, felt less secure and more willing to participate in their common defence. At the same time, they were more afraid of not being able to face the WTO forces without sufficient US participation. They decided not to reduce their military spending, whereas the US Senate abandoned plans to withdraw US troops from Europe.[71]

In the communist camp, Operation Danube had multiple and largely negative consequences. Although Czechoslovakia was firmly held by the Kremlin, the Western Communist Parties who condemned the invasion moved away from Moscow and embarked on the adventure of Eurocommunism in the 1970s. The Brezhnev Doctrine, which stated that the USSR and its allies had the duty to intervene in the internal affairs of a state within their sphere of influence if socialism was threatened there, appeared in 1968 to give a theoretical justification to Operation Danube. The invasion had many consequences. First, it finalised the Sino–Soviet split, as Beijing feared that the Soviet Union would use the doctrine as a justification to invade or interfere with Chinese communism; this pushed Beijing to move closer to Washington in 1972. Also, 11 years after invasion of Czechoslovakia, it justified in 1979 the Soviet intervention in Afghanistan which played a crucial role in the crisis and the eventual demise of the USSR.

By an irony of history, when Gorbachev wished to reform the Soviet Union from 1985, he was influenced by Dubček's "socialism with a human face". During his studies in Moscow in the early 1950s, he became a friend of Zdenek Mlynar, who would be one of the main animators of the Prague Spring, and they met extensively in 1967.[72] Gorbachev's reforms, as Brezhnev had feared for Czechoslovakia, eventually led to the disappearance of the USSR and the whole Eastern Bloc.

Selected Bibliography

Bartosek, Karel, *Les Aveux des archives, Prague-Paris-Prague, 1948–1968* (Le Seuil, 1996).

Bischof, Günther, Karner, Stefan and Ruggenthaler, Peter, *The Prague Spring and the Warsaw Pact invasion of Czechoslovakia in 1968* (Lexington Books, 2010).

Číțek, Martin, *Vojensko-politické aspekty sovětské invaze do ČSSR v srpnu 1968* (Univerzita Karlova v Praze, 2013).

Courtois, Stéphane, *Le livre noir du communisme* (Robert Laffont, 1998).

Crump, Laura Carolien, *The Warsaw Pact Reconsidered* (Universiteit Utrecht, 2014).

Desgraupe, Pierre and Dumayet, Pierre, *Prague, l'été des tanks* (Tchou, 1968).

Dubcek, Alexandre, *C'est l'espoir qui meurt en dernier, Autobiographie* (Paris: Editions Fayard, 1993).

Fejtö, François, *Histoire des démocraties populaires. 2, Après Staline 1953–1971* (Point-Seuil, 1971).

Fowkes, Ben, *Eastern Europe 1945–1969: From Stalinism to Stagnation* (Longman, 2000).

Guth, Robert M., *The Soviet Decision to Invade Czechoslovakia* (Rand Corporation, 1975).

Hottman, Aleš and Mackovic, Stanislav, 'Rudé hvězdy nad Československem 1968–1991 Část 1', http://www.vrtulnik.cz/mil3/invaze.pdf.

Hrdina III, Otakar, *Study of Civil-Military Relations in Crises of Czechoslovak History* (Naval Postgraduate School, 2005).

Johnson, Ross A., Dean, Robert W. and Alexiev, Alexander, *East European Military Establishments: The Warsaw Pact Northern Tier* (Rand Corporation, 1980).

Kaplan, Karel, *Dans les Archives du comité central: Trente ans de secrets du bloc soviétique* (Albin Michel, 1978).

Kramer, Mark, 'The Prague Spring and the Soviet Invasion of Czechoslovakia. New Interpretations', *Cold War International History Project Bulletin*, Issue 3 (Fall 1993).

Křivancová, Jana, *Okupace Československa 1968* (Západočeská univerzita v Plzni, 2013).

Lavrenov, Serguei and Popov, Igor, *Sovetskiy Soyuz v lokal'nykh voynakh i konfliktakh* (Astrel, 2003).

Lecomte, Bernard, *Gorbatchev* (Perrin, 2014).

Lůnák, Petr, 'Planning for Nuclear War: The Czechoslovak War Plan of 1964', *Cold War International History Project Bulletin*, Issue 12/13 (Fall/Winter 2001).

Mahoney, William, M., *The history of the Czech Republic and Slovakia* (Greenwood, 2011).

Mayorov, Aleksandr, *Vtorzheniye. Chekhoslovakiya. 1968* (Prava Cheloveka, 1998).

Mlynar, Zdenek, Fritsch-Estrangin, Guy and Gaillard-Paquet, Jean-Marie, *Le Froid vient de Moscou: Prague 1968, du socialisme réel au socialisme à visage humain* (Gallimard, 1981).

Navazelskis, Ina, *Alexander Dubcek* (Chelsea House Publications, 1990).

Navratíl, Jaromir et al. (eds), *The Prague Spring 1968: A National Security Archive Documents Reader* (Budapest: Central European University Press, 1998).

Novak, Miroslav, *Du printemps de Prague au printemps de Moscou* (Lug, 1990).

Okorokov, Aleksandr, *Sekretnyye voyny Sovetskogo Soyuza* (Eksmo, 2013).

Ouimet, Matthew, *The Rise and Fall of the Brezhnev Doctrine in Soviet Foreign Policy* (University of North Carolina Press, 2003).

Pikhoya, R.G., 'Chekhoslovakiya, 1968 god. Vzglyad iz Moskvy. Po dokumentam TSK KPSS', *Novaya i noveyshaya istoriya*, no. 6 (1994).

Povolný, Daniel, *Vojenské řešení Pražského jara, Invaze armád Varšavské smlouvy* (Agentura vojenských informací a služeb, 2008).

Pucik, Miloslav, 'The Military Occupation of Slovakia in August 1968 and Its Consequences', in *International Cold War Military Records and History: Proceedings of the International Conference on Cold War Military Records* (US Army Center of Military History, 1996).

Rice, Condoleezza, *The Soviet Union and the Czechoslovak Army, 1948–1983: Uncertain Allegiance* (Princeton University Press, 2014).

Rogoza, Serguei and Achkasov, Nikolai, *Zasekrechennyye voyny. 1950–2000 gg* (Poligon, 2003).

Salomon, Michel, *Prague, la révolution étranglée* (Robert Laffont, 1968).

Shevchenko, Viraly, *Navstrechu rassvetu* (Altaîr, 2011).

Skilling, Gordon H., *Czechoslovakia's Interrupted Revolution* (Princeton University Press, 1976).

Stolarik, Mark (ed.), *The 'Prague Spring' and the Warsaw Pact Invasion of Czechoslovakia, 1968: Forty Years Later* (Bolchazy-Carducci Publishers, 2010).

Valenta, Jiri, *Soviet Intervention in Czechoslovakia, 1968: Anatomy of a Decision* (Johns Hopkins University Press, 1979).

Volkogonov, Dmitri, *Sem' vozhdey. Kn.2* (Novosti, 1995).

Williams, Kieran, *The Prague Spring and its Aftermath: Czechoslovak Politics, 1968–1970* (Cambridge University Press, 1997).

Windsor, Philip and Roberts, Adam, *Czechoslovakia 1968: Reform, Repression and Resistance* (Columbia University Press, 1969).

Much additional information was obtained from online sources of reference such as armada.vojenstvi.cz, armedconflicts.com, csla.cz, digitalarchives.wilsoncenter.org and dunay1968.com.

Notes

Chapter 1
1. William M. Mahoney, The History of the Czech Republic and Slovakia (Greenwood, 2011), p.53.
2. Mahoney, p.74.
3. Mahoney, p.136.
4. Aleksandr Okorokov, Sekretnyye voyny Sovetskogo Soyuza (Eksmo, 2013), p.628.
5. Nigel Thomas, Foreign Volunteers of the Allied Forces 1939–45 (Osprey Publishing, 1998), p.5.
6. Okorokov, p.629.
7. Okorokov, p.630.
8. Okorokov, p.633.
9. Okorokov, p.633.

Chapter 2
1. Karel Bartosek, Les Aveux des archives, Prague–Paris–Prague, 1948–1968 (Le Seuil, 1996).
2. Michel Salomon, Prague, la révolution étranglée (Robert Laffont, 1968), pp.246–47.
3. Salomon, p.251.
4. Salomon, p.144.

5   Salomon, p.183.
6   Karel Kaplan, Dans les Archives du comité central: Trente ans de secrets du bloc soviétique (Albin Michel, 1978), pp.165–66.
7   Ross Johnson, Robert W. Dean & Alexander Alexiev, East European Military Establishments: The Warsaw Pact Northern Tier (Rand Corporation, 1980), p.157.
8   Martin Čítek, Vojensko-politické aspekty sovětské invaze do ČSSR v srpnu 1968 (Univerzita Karlova v Praze, 2013), p.59.
9   Johnson, et al, p.135.
10 Daniel Povolný, Vojenské řešení Pražského jara, Invaze armád Varšavské smlouvy (Agentura vojenských informací a služeb, 2008), pp. 148–49.
11 Miloslav Pucik, 'The Military Occupation of Slovakia in August 1968 and Its Consequences', in International Cold War Military Records and History: Proceedings of the International Conference on Cold War Military Records (US Army Center of Military History, 1996), p.499.
12 Aleš Hottman & Stanislav Mackovic, http://www.vrtulnik.cz/mil3/invaze.pdf, p.1.
13 Contemporary planning envisaged the deployment of the Soviet 57th Air Army (from the Carpathian Military District) to Czechoslovakia in the case of a war with the NATO. Renamed the 14th Air Army in 1968, this included one fighter aviation division, one fighter-bomber aviation division, two bomber aviation regiments, and one reconnaissance aviation regiment. Upon moving into Czechoslovakia, these were expected to integrate units of the 10th Air Army, and then systematically seek and destroy enemy nuclear weapons, air bases, and command nodes, before providing close air support to ground forces (Eastern Order of Battle, 'Soviet Carpathian Miltiary District's 57th (14th) Tactical Air Army, 1 January 1968', 15 August 2020, www.easternorbat.com
14 Povolný, p.149 & Eastern Order of Battle, 'Czechoslovak People's Army: Air Force Command, 10th Air Army, 1968', 26 July 2020, www.easternorbat.com,
15 Kieran Williams, The Prague Spring and its Aftermath: Czechoslovak Politics, 1968–1970 (Cambridge University Press, 1997), p.116.
16 Johnson, et al, p.154.
17 http://armada.vojenstvi.cz/povalecna/studie/7.htm.
18 The USSR, Bulgaria, Poland, the GDR, Hungary, Romania and Albania, who left the alliance in September 1968.
19 Čítek, p.16.
20 Čítek, p.80.
21 Čítek, pp.22–23.
22 Pucik, p.500.
23 Cold War International History Project Bulletin, Issue 12/13, pp.290–98.
24 Johnson, et al, p.137.
25 Čítek, p.83.
26 Čítek, p.32.
27 Čítek, p.81.
28 Mark Kramer, 'The Prague Spring and the Soviet Invasion of Czechoslovakia. New Interpretations', Cold War International History Project Bulletin, Issue 3 (Fall 1993), p.9.
29 Čítek, pp.24–25.
30 Čítek, p.53.

Chapter 3
1   Husak, a member of the KSČ since 1929, was the strongman of Slovakia from 1945–49. He was arrested in 1951, tortured and sentenced to life imprisonment. He was liberated in 1960 before becoming one of the representatives of the Slovak communist reformers in Bratislava.
2   François Fejtö, Histoire des démocraties populaires. 2, Après Staline 1953–1971 (Point-Seuil, 1971), pp.193–94.
3   Williams, p.170.
4   Salomon, pp.20–23.
5   Le Monde (13 November 1967).
6   Jana Křivancová, Okupace Československa 1968 (Západočeská univerzita v Plzni, 2013), p.13.
7   Williams, p.54.
8   Křivancová, p.14.
9   Johnson, et al, p.146.
10 Janko committed suicide on 14 March 1968, leaving a diary that provided details of the coup organised by Šejna.
11 Salomon, pp.52–55.
12 Williams, p.64.
13 Křivancová, p.14.
14 Křivancová, p.15.
15 Okorokov, p.636.
16 Serguei Lavrenov & Igor Popov, Sovetskiy Soyuz v lokal'nykh voynakh i konfliktakh (Astrel, 2003), p.293.
17 Křivancová, p.15.
18 Williams, p.68.
19 Williams, p.68.
20 Pierre Desgraupe & Pierre Dumayet, Prague, l'été des tanks (Tchou, 1968), p.55.
21 Salomon, p.187.
22 Williams, p.74.
23 Salomon, p.84.
24 Desgraupe & Dumayet, p.55.
25 Salomon, pp.249–53.
26 Pucik, p.504.
27 Williams, p.156.
28 Williams, p.83.
29 Čítek, p.60.
30 Čítek, p. 71.
31 Johnson, et al, p. 149.
32 Čítek, p. 70.
33 Čítek, p.63.
34 Johnson, et al, p.140.
35 Johnson, pp.140–41.
36 Daniel Samek, Srpnová invaze do Československa roku 1968 v Brně (Univerzita Karlova v Praze, 2011), p.13.
37 Lavrenov & Popov, p.296.
38 Lavrenov & Popov, p.296.
39 Williams, pp.87–89.

Chapter 4
1   Williams, p.66.
2   Williams, p.66.
3   Williams, p.33.
4   Robert M. Guth, The Soviet Decision to Invade Czechoslovakia (Rand Corporation, 1975), p.13.
5   Lavrenov & Popov, p.300.
6   Okorokov, p.636.
7   R.G. Pikhoya, 'Chekhoslovakiya, 1968 god. Vzglyad iz Moskvy. Po dokumentam TSK KPSS', Novaya i noveyshaya istoriya, no. 6 (1994), p.9.
8   Williams, p.71.
9   Günter Bischof, Stefan Karner & Peter Ruggenthaler, The Prague Spring and the Warsaw Pact Invasion of Czechoslovakia in 1968 (Lexington Books, 2010), p.6.
10 Bischof, et al, p.7.
11 Laura Carolien Crump, The Warsaw Pact Reconsidered (Universiteit Utrecht, 2014), pp.260–262.
12 Williams, p.71.
13 Henri-Christian Giraud, L'Accord secret de Baden-Baden (Rocher, 2018), p.16.
14 Okorokov, p.643.
15 Bischof, et al, p.10.
16 Křivancová, p.27.
17 Okorokov, p.649.
18 Čítek, pp.98–99.
19 Čítek, p.97.
20 Williams, p.33.
21 Okorokov, p.644.
22 Okorokov, p.644.
23 Bischof, et al, p.12.
24 Okorokov, p.644.
25 Crump, pp.267–68.
26 Williams, pp.77–78.
27 Křivancová, p.25.
28 During the Czechoslovak crisis, the GDR, USSR, Poland, Bulgaria and Hungary were called 'the Five'.
29 Williams, pp.115–16.
30 Povolný, p.22.
31 Guth, pp.20–21
32 Č'tek, p.100.
33 Hottman & Mackovic, p.2.
34 Williams, p.116.
35 Čítek, p.103.
36 Lavrenov & Popov, p.315.
37 Okorokov, p.643.
38 Okorokov, p.643.
39 Williams, p.117.
40 Křivancová, p.29.
41 Pikhoya, p.16.
42 Pucik, pp.504–05.
43 Povolný, p.36.
44 Hottman & Mackovic, p.2.
45 Povolný, p.47.
46 Lavrenov & Popov, p.317.
47 Crump, p.274.
48 Čítek, p.115.
49 Povolný, p.74.
50 Williams, p.92.
51 Williams, p.94.
52 Lavrenov & Popov, p.309.
53 Williams, p.116.
54 Lavrenov & Popov, p.320.
55 Williams, p.118.

56 Lavrenov & Popov, p.320.
57 Pikhoya, p.16.
58 Čítek, p.94.
59 Kramer, p.8.
60 Čítek, p.96.
61 Williams, p.121.
62 Hottman & Mackovic, p.1.
63 Čítek, p.123.
64 Čítek, p.124.
65 Povolný, p.76.
66 Povolný, pp.76–77.
67 Lavrenov & Popov, p.321.
68 Čítek, p.121.
69 Křivancová, p.36.
70 Williams, p.100.
71 Křivancová, p.35.
72 S. Lavrenov & I. Popov, p. 310.
73 Křivancová, p.36.
74 Křivancová, p.37.
75 Crump, p.285.

Chapter 5
1 Čítek, p.86.
2 Williams, p.111.
3 Čítek, p.89.
4 Čítek, p.89.
5 S. Lavrenov & I. Popov, p.321.
6 Okorokov, p.646.
7 Dmitri Volkogonov, *Sem' vozhdey. Kn.2* (Novosti, 1995), p.46.
8 Williams, p.121.
9 Křivancová, p.38.
10 Williams, p.104.
11 Williams, p.105.
12 Williams, p.109.
13 Křivancová, p.40.
14 Williams, pp.106–07.
15 Povolný, p. 77.
16 Serguei Rogoza & Nikolai Achkasov, *Zasekrechennyye voyny. 1950–2000 gg* (Poligon, 2003), p.283.
17 Williams, p.110.
18 Williams, p.125.
19 Crump, p.289.
20 Rogoza & Achkasov, p.287.
21 Aleksandr Mayorov, *Vtorzheniye. Chekhoslovakiya. 1968* (Prava Cheloveka, 1998). pp.218–19.
22 Bischof, et al, p.24.
23 Rogoza & Achkasov, p.300.
24 Vitaliy Shevchenko, *Navstrechu rassvetu* (Altaîr, 2011), p.40.
25 Čítek, p.131.
26 Williams, p.122.
27 Williams, p.123.
28 Guth, p.33.
29 Samek, pp.18–19.
30 Čítek, p.133.
31 Williams, p.128.
32 Williams, p.219.
33 Johnson, et al, p.142.
34 Křivancová, p.53.
35 Lavrenov & Popov, pp.325–26.
36 Čítek, p.135.
37 Samek, p.18.
38 Čítek, p.135.
39 Křivancová, p.49.
40 Williams, p.126.
41 Williams, p.127.
42 Křivancová, p. 58.
43 *ČTK* was the official Czechoslovak news agency.
44 Williams, p. 126.
45 Crump, p. 290.
46 Křivancová, p. 59.
47 Williams, p.131.
48 Williams, p.127.
49 Křivancová, p.62.

Chapter 6
1 Povolný, p.98
2 Okorokov, p.650.
3 Okorokov, p.650.
4 Povolný, p.99.
5 Shevchenko, p.56.
6 Hottman & Mackovic, p.2.
7 Rogoza & Achkasov, p.288.
8 Hottman & Mackovic, p.3.
9 Čítek, pp.140–41. By way of comparison, Germany lined up 3,580 tanks against the USSR during Operation Barbarossa, and Czechoslovakia had a population of just under 15 million.
10 Okorokov, p.653.
11 Hottman & Mackovic, p.1.
12 Povolný, p.94.
13 Orders given by the Soviet staff for Operation Danube were issued by the Moscow time zone. It might be that the NVA did not take into account the two-hour gap between the Moscow and Central European time zones. This scheduling problem also surprised Dubček's opponents at the KSČ Central Committee on 20 August, who were caught out by the announcement of the invasion.
14 The BND, or Bundesnachrichtendienst (Federal Intelligence Service), was the foreign intelligence agency of West Germany.
15 Hottman & Mackovic, p.2.
16 Povolný, p.100.
17 Povolný, p.100.
18 S. Rogoza & N. Achkasov, p.290.
19 Povolný, p.101.
20 Rogoza & Achkasov, p.292.
21 Hottman & Mackovic, p.5.
22 Povolný, p.102.
23 Povolný, p.102.
24 Povolný, p.102.
25 30 June, 1967 Commander of the airborne forces, then again Colonel General V.F. Margelov, approved his designs for a new uniform for paratroopers, including two berets. The everyday uniform was supposed to wear a khaki beret with a red star. However, this beret has remained on paper. [Facing] the drawing of a burgundy beret, Margelov put a resolution: "Leave for the parades in Moscow". On the right side of the beret there was a blue flag with the emblem of the airborne forces, and in front of it there was a star in a crown of ears [?]. The officers wore a cockade with the emblem of the 1955 model and a flight emblem (a star with wings). Burgundy berets began arriving with supply troops in August-September 1967. During the military parade of 7 November 1967, for the first time, paratroopers in new uniforms and berets marched through Red Square.
At the origin of this re-equipment was General I.I. Lisov, a veteran of the airborne forces, who … introduced a blue beret. The initiative found the warm approval of Margelova, because the first experiences showed that the soldiers liked the beret.
In a burgundy beret, soldiers of the 317th Guards Regiment of the 103rd Vitebsk Guards Airborne Division entered Czechoslovakia in August 1968. However, soldiers of the 7th Airborne Guards Division from Kaunas, wore already blue berets and, judging by eyewitness accounts, the locals initially mistook them for representatives of the UN troops, http://crimea-vdv.ru/?p=20648
26 Hottman & Mackovic, p.3.
27 Rogoza & Achkasov, p.296.
28 Křivancová, p.64.
29 Povolný, p.104.
30 Povolný, p.102.
31 Hottman & Mackovic, p.2.
32 Williams, p.127.
33 S. Rogoza & N. Achkasov, p.293.
34 Povolný, p.107.
35 Povolný, p.109.
36 Povolný, p.109.
37 Povolný, p.110.
38 Povolný, p.110.
39 Povolný, pp.111–12.
40 Povolný, p.113.
41 Povolný, p.111.
42 Hottman & Mackovic, p.4.
43 Hottman & Mackovic, p.3.
44 Povolný, p.115.
45 Povolný, p.116.
46 Povolný, pp.115–16.
47 Hottman & Mackovic, p.9.
48 Povolný, p.119.
49 Povolný, p.119.
50 Povolný, p.119.
51 Povolný, p.120.
52 Povolný, p.121.
53 Povolný, p.121.
54 Rogoza & Achkasov, pp.297–98.
55 Povolný, p.121.
56 Povolný, p.122.
57 Povolný, p.123.
58 Povolný, p.124.
59 Povolný, p.125.

Acknowledgements

This book would not have been possible without the help and support of many people. I would first like to thank Tom Cooper, Andy Miles, and Albert Grandolini for their help, but also the entire Helion team, without whom this book would not have been possible.

I also want to thank all my friends from Strasbourg, who encouraged me in writing this book, and the patience of my daughter Sasha.

About the Author

David Francois, from France, earned his PhD in Contemporary History at the University of Burgundy and specialised in studying militant communism, its military history and the relationship between politics and violence in contemporary history. In 2009, he co-authored the *Guide des archives de l'Internationale communiste* published by the French National Archives and the Maison des sciences de l'Homme in Dijon. He regularly contributes articles for various French military history magazines and is also a regular contributor to the French history website L'autre côté de la colline. This is his fourth book for the @War series.

60 Povolný, p.123.
61 Povolný, p.126.
62 Williams, p.136.
63 Hottman & Mackovic, p.3.
64 Samek, pp.17–18.
65 Hottman & Mackovic, p.4.
66 Samek, p.22.
67 Hottman & Mackovic, p.4.
68 Povolný, p.129.
69 Čížek, p.142.
70 Hottman & Mackovic, p.4.
71 Povolný, p.5.
72 Rogoza & Achkasov, p.300.
73 Ministers of the USSR, was considered as 'Brezhnev's man' in Prague; Bischof, Karner & Ruggenthaler, p.8.
74 Williams, p.124.

Chapter 7
1 Williams, p.127.
2 Samek, p.21.
3 Shevchenko, p.77.
4 Křivancová, p.68.
5 Williams, p.129.
6 Křivancová, p.68.
7 Emil Hácha was President of the Czechoslovak Republic during the German occupation, and Emil Moravec a Nazi collaborator.
8 Křivancová, p.69.
9 Otakar Hrdina III, *Study of Civil-Military Relations in Crises of Czechoslovak History* (Naval Postgraduate School, 2005), p.44.
10 Rogoza & Achkasov, p.298.
11 The teaching of the Russian language was compulsory at school, which explains the ease of communication between the Czechoslovakian population and the Soviet soldiers.
12 https://www.radio.cz/fr/rubrique/histoire/le-jeune-archeologue-francais-et-linvasion-de-la-tchecoslovaquie.
13 Křivancová, p.71.
14 Rogoza & Achkasov, p.301.
15 Okorokov, pp.656–57.
16 Okorokov, p.657.
17 Rogoza & Achkasov, p.290.
18 Povolný, p.130.
19 Povolný, p.134.
20 Povolný, p.133.
21 Povolný, p.134.
22 Povolný, p.135.
23 Povolný, p.136.
24 Chkalovsky was an air base about 30km northeast of Moscow.
25 Hottman & Mackovic, p.6.
26 Křivancová, p.71.
27 Bischof, et al, p.219.
28 Povolný, p.99.
29 Povolný, p.99.
30 Křivancová, p.64.
31 Křivancová, p.65.
32 Williams, p.133.
33 Křivancová, p.66.
34 Křivancová, pp.73–74.
35 Guth, p.38.
36 Williams, p.135.
37 Křivancová, p.86.
38 Křivancová, p.76.
39 Williams, p.138.
40 Williams, p.138.
41 Křivancová, p.78.
42 Williams, p.141.
43 Křivancová, p.80.
44 Williams, pp.142–43.
45 Křivancová, p.81.
46 Čížek, p.146.
47 Okorokov, p.658.
48 Okorokov, p.660.
49 Pucik, p.512.
50 Čížek, p.147.
51 Williams, p.158.
52 Williams, p.158.
53 Williams, p.168.
54 Kramer, p.10.
55 Crump, p.299.
56 Čížek, pp.148–149.
57 Čížek, p.157.
58 Rogoza & Achkasov, p.306.
59 Husak also became President of the Republic in 1975.
60 Williams, p.47.
61 Williams, pp.242–243.
62 Williams, p.160.
63 Williams, p.47.
64 Stéphane Courtois (ed.), *Le livre noir du communisme* (Robert Laffont, 1998), p.513.
65 Williams, p.237.
66 Williams, p.174.
67 Čížek, p.162.
68 Rogoza & Achkasov, p.307.
69 Bischof, et al, p.25.
70 https://www.nytimes.com/2007/10/01/world/europe/01czech.html.
71 Williams, pp.226–27.
72 Bernard Lecomte, *Gorbatchev* (Perrin, 2014), pp.33–34.